T0356178

A Caring Family

PRAISE FOR *A CARING FAMILY*

If you are looking for a book on family that will challenge and inspire you, look no further!

Mark Batterson, *NYT* best-selling author of *The Circle Maker*

Aaron is a gifted storyteller. He has a gentle self-deprecation that is humorous, transparent, and insightful. Joyfully he proposes ways and means for the very serious work of caring for our families. If the family is destroyed, or self-destructs, there is no hope for society or the world. I recommend *A Caring Family* to you, for it brims with hope of what our families can beautifully be. I have learned much from the practical wisdom of this delightfully written book and enjoyed chuckling my way through it—as I am confident will you.

Dick Brogden, co-founder of the Live Dead Movement, Dubai, UAE

Aaron provides well-researched content, adventurous and engaging stories, and thought-provoking questions to help your family grow in how they care for one another and begin building a family mindset that prioritizes people because of their God-given dignity.

Jon Gordon, fifteen-times bestselling author

After reading *A Caring Family*, one word comes to mind: prophylaxis. During our years in Africa, our family took a malaria prophylaxis as a preventative treatment. Although the efficacy of the treatment was not a guarantee, it helped. For those just starting a family or somewhere on the journey, putting Aaron's seven virtues into practice is like taking a prophylaxis: a preventative treatment against misplaced priorities and missed opportunities to model caring. In other words, it can save you from experiencing regret for what you did or did not do for those you love the most, setting an example your children can follow.

Pastor Boyd Powers

Aaron does a brilliant job of drawing on personal experience, his own family history, and the wisdom of learned professionals to create a user-friendly guidebook to becoming a more caring family member. His passion for the subject is evident in every chapter as he weaves a tapestry well worthy of the time investment in the read. To my fellow West Virginia brother, bravo!

Dr. Butch Frey

As I read *A Caring Family* I found myself pulled into the life stories, asking myself head and heart questions at the end of each chapter that helped me see areas I could grow that will impact my family, and looking forward to engaging in the skill practices laid out at the end of each chapter. This is a must-read that will change you and your family.

Pastor Sam Farina

A Caring Family is another home run from my good friend, Dr. Aaron Santmyire! All of us know we need to do more to genuinely care for those around us, but knowing where to start and how to proceed can be a challenge. Filled with practical applications and personal stories of encouragement, you'll find a number of strategies for your journey in this hope-filled book. And enough plugs for West Virginia that you might even be tempted to relocate your family to this fine state! Read *A Caring Family*, let God instill the principles deep into your soul, and you'll be well on your way to caring for those around you like you've always wanted to.

Pastor Doug Seaman

A Caring Family is a powerful guide for cultivating healthy family relationships. Using great stories, insightful principles, and practical application, Aaron Santmyire helps you implement seven essential ingredients to develop a caring family.

Stephen Blandino, lead pastor, 7 City Church, and author of *Stop Chasing Easy*

As a father and husband of over thirty years, and a global missionary, *A Caring Family* by Aaron Santmyire resonates deeply with my own journey and experiences. Santmyire's book is not just a collection of words on pages; it's a profound reflection on the virtues that underpin the strength of a family's love and connection. Santmyire's call for an intentional family life centered around seven virtues is a message that reverberates in my soul. I can't help but reflect on the lessons I wish I had known when my wife and I were raising our children, lessons that could have enriched our family life. The book is, in many ways, a heartfelt letter to my younger self, offering valuable insights that can shape the future of family relationships. This book is a source of inspiration and a testament to the enduring bonds that make a family truly special.

Danny W. Davis, Ed.D.

Reading *A Caring Family* is like attending a science lecture, counseling session, theology class, and revival meeting all at the same time. Practicality is the name of the game. This book gives you concepts and strategies and doable tracks to run on. Aaron's personal transparency, stories with a dozen twists, and takeaways are simply a gift. What else would you expect from a husband, father, PhD in Nursing, and decades of work in Africa? I love it!

Dick Foth, author, *A Trip Around the Sun* and *Known: Finding Deep Friendships in a Shallow World*

A Caring Family gifts us with fresh vision for building and nurturing healthy, caring families regardless of what stage you are in. Written with insightful research, real life stories, and opportunities for reflection with those you love, Aaron masterfully provides a roadmap for shifting our family relationships and thereby, influencing our communities for the greater good.

Kadi Cole, leadership consultant, executive coach, and author of *Developing Female Leaders*

A Caring Family is an exceptional tool that encourages health, wholeness, and transformation. Through story and transparency, the author introduces seven traits that create a path for families to emulate and grow together. As a lover of spiritual and personal transformation, I highly recommend this book. It will change your life personally and transform your family.

> **Lisa Potter,** author of *The Collective Journey* and executive director of Women Who Lead

A Caring Family is a conversational and practical book that's a must-read for any parent who wants to raise children who love people well. This book will guide you on a journey of looking at timeless values that, when intentionally instilled in the home, create a ripple effect that reaches far and wide. And, it gives you an easy-to-follow roadmap to do that.

> **Lauren Wells**, CEO of Unstacking Company

In his own unique way, Aaron (or Dr. Aaron Santmyire) weaves the stories of his life into the story of our lives. As a father, grandfather, and spiritual father to many, *A Caring Family* has impacted me in unexpected ways with its humility, honesty, and life-giving principles. As you read and embrace the powerful truths of *A Caring Family* you will be challenged to pause and take an inventory of the Seven Virtues that Aaron articulates as keys to a healthy caring family. You will see how each one of these virtues is or is not being lived out in your family or the families that you influence. No matter what your circumstance or stage in life, this book is a must, not only to read, but to put in practice for your family and all those who you can touch with its truths.

> **Pastor Mark Lehmann,** Cornerstone Church

Aaron Santmyire's witty wordsmithing and authentic storytelling enhance the much-needed message of this book. We all want our lives to count for eternity. We want our family to play a pivotal role in God's grand narrative. Thankfully, *A Caring Family* is here to help you thrive in your God-given calling. Through resonating stories, practical tips, and reflective questions, Santmyire provides the tools you and your family need to live a robust, gospel-centered, soul-winning lifestyle. Read this book, receive its inspiration, respond to the challenge, and ready your loved ones to become people who know God's heart and, as a result, naturally long to join his mission.

David Joannes, founder/CEO of Within Reach Global and author of *The Mind of a Missionary* and *See the City*

Being a care pastor during this unique time, has been challenging. Dr. Santmyire's book, *A Caring Life,* came at a perfect time to help equip Care Ministry servants in relating in love to those being served and those we are serving with. I am so excited to share Dr. Santmyire's second book, *A Caring Family,* with those who serve the body of Christ. Anyone who has committed themselves faithfully to Kingdom service for a period of time is well aware the "enemy of our souls" believes attacking the family is one of the best tactics to totally sideline the Lord's people from service. *A Caring Family* is a great resource to equip everyone in a family as they live out the Lord's priorities for loving and caring for one another. I believe there is no social structure stronger than a loving family serving the Lord.

Pastor Arnold Bracy, Cornerstone Church

A Caring Family

SEVEN VIRTUES
THAT HELP YOUR FAMILY
CARE BETTER AND LOVE LONGER

Dr. Aaron Santmyire

NEW YORK

LONDON • NASHVILLE • MELBOURNE • VANCOUVER

A Caring Family

Seven Virtues that Your Family Care Better and Love Longer

Published in New York, New York by Entre Pastors Press, an Imprint of Morgan James Publishing. Morgan James is a trademark of Morgan James, LLC.

Scripture taken from THE HOLY BIBLE, NEW INTERNATIONAL VERSION ®. Copyright© 1973, 1978, 1984, 2011 by Biblica, Inc.™. Used by permission of Zondervan.

Proudly distributed by Publishers Group West®

A FREE ebook edition is available for you or a friend with the purchase of this print book.

CLEARLY SIGN YOUR NAME ABOVE

Instructions to claim your free ebook edition:
1. Visit MorganJamesBOGO.com
2. Sign your name CLEARLY in the space above
3. Complete the form and submit a photo of this entire page
4. You or your friend can download the ebook to your preferred device

ISBN 9781636984568 paperback
ISBN 9781636984575 ebook
Library of Congress Control Number: 2024933880

Cover and Interior Design by:
Chris Treccani
www.3dogcreative.net

Morgan James is a proud partner of Habitat for Humanity Peninsula and Greater Williamsburg. Partners in building since 2006.

Get involved today! Visit: www.morgan-james-publishing.com/giving-back

To Heather, Isabelle, and Josiah.
You have taught me more about a *caring family*
than anyone else.

Thanks for loving me when I am AAron and when I am Ron.

CONTENTS

FOREWORD

This book is like no other family book I've ever read. Dr. Aaron Santmyire absolutely intrigues me. He is a master storyteller, and in this book he will become a friend and mentor to you. Like Aaron himself, this book is deep, insightful, vulnerable, engaging, intentional, and yes, caring. While most family books are written from the viewpoint of a family counselor or expert, this book is written by a deeply curious learner who happens to be a missionary currently living in Africa, a husband, father, son, brother, nurse practitioner and avid sleepwalker. (He will tell you more about that phenomenon in the book.)

While reading *A Caring Family*, you will not only become familiar with Aaron and his family, but you will also be captivated by the way he unravels a narrative and draws you in. The best communicators I know are great storytellers. Jesus was a genius at making a common story come alive to change your perspective and life. Many of the stories in this book will help you understand a concept and principle that is life changing. Aaron describes himself as a habit, rhythm, and discipline guy. There is no doubt about this when you consider the fact that he reads more books in a month than most individuals do in a year. He listens to more podcasts in a month than some do in a lifetime. No wonder *The Clarity Podcast* is so excellent. The combination of Aaron's life experience, love for learning, intentionality, and ability to connect is incredible. I first met Aaron as a guest on his podcast, and it felt like we had been lifelong friends. That same sense of connection will permeate through the pages of this book when you read it.

After reading this manuscript, it prompted me to consider my own family and reflect upon the significance of caring. Since the family environment is often where compassion is nurtured, it made me question if my wife, Cathy, and I have been deliberate in instilling the value of caring in our own children. It reminded me of my wife, who excels in displaying caring and generosity far more than I do. I realized much of what Aaron is writing about is "more caught than taught." Cathy has the spiritual gift of giving. Recently, the deadliest wildfire in modern US history happened in Maui, Hawaii. We have a friend, more like an acquaintance, whose family lost their home. Somehow my wife found out there was a "GoFundMe" site for this woman. My wife asked me to send a donation. When I looked to see the list of who else had given, I noticed that all three of my daughters were among the contributors. I shouldn't have been surprised, but I guess I was and realized Cathy had done a good job of showing our kids how to care and serve by her lifestyle.

Too many times when I read a book about family, I feel discouraged, rather than energized. Not this one. Aaron's openness and vulnerability about his own life inspire me to strive for greater intentionality in embracing the seven virtues he discusses in this book. Being involved in the medical field, when you support someone during their final moments or console a grieving spouse, it's impossible not to be profoundly impacted by the experience. Aaron has exemplified this, and he serves as an inspiration for us to cultivate these virtues within our own lives and families. This book will help you and your family become a safe place to share healthy emotions and live a caring family life.

Jim Burns, PhD
President, HomeWord
Author of *Doing Life with Your Adult Children:*
Keep Your Mouth Shut and the Welcome Mat Out

PREFACE

As many already know, I am a strong advocate for all homemade apple pies. A great homemade apple pie is my favorite food on earth, no questions asked. An apple pie requires a specific recipe, quality ingredients, and precise instructions. You heat the oven to the required temperature, roll out the crust, prepare the apples and filling of the pie, and with love put the pie together. Even with all this intentionality, the apple pie, in my opinion, never tastes the same. The texture, juiciness, or hardness of the apples may be different, the cinnamon might be weaker or stronger, or the consistency and quality of the flour may cause the crust to be extra crispy or super flaky. In my apple pie connoisseur experience, there are always differences even if you use the same recipe.

I know you are not reading this book for me to share the intricacies of making or eating an apple pie. But as a husband and parent, one thing I have spent considerable time on is searching for a "recipe" of sorts on how to have a healthy, caring family environment and how to raise kids who love Jesus and care for others with the love of Jesus, a family which is not given into the constant cultural messages of being self-focused, but one that deeply understands that the more you focus on yourself or ourselves, the smaller our world and life becomes.

To that end, I have read more books and listened to more podcasts about the family, all the while thinking I would find the recipe. Amongst the words I have read and thousands upon thousands of words I have listened to, I have learned many helpful ideas and tips. But I still have not found the recipe that works every time to produce a caring family.

At times, I can be slow to catch on. And it took me a while to realize that the recipe I was looking for did not exist. It logically makes sense that if recipes used for making apple pies do not turn out the same, why would I think there would be one for living things with a free will? And I have become convinced that even if parents and families model for family members what it means to love Jesus and care for others with the love of Jesus, ultimately individuals choose for themselves. I frequently pray this prayer that I first heard from Reggie Campbell. It goes like this, "That God would give me wisdom to know what to do, the courage to do it, and the faith to trust Him with the outcomes."[1]

A caring family is one of those faith building experiences of trusting Jesus with the outcomes.

Maybe you are a parent who has tried to instill the values of caring in your children, and it has not worked out as you thought it would. Or maybe your kids have turned out to be the most caring people in the world. I remember Dr. James Dobson sharing, in one of the thousands of podcasts I have listened to, something to the effect that parents whose children are healthy and turning out the way they wanted them to take too much of the credit, and parents who raise children who are not turning out the way they wanted them to take too much of the blame. He shared that the reality is somewhere between these extremes.[2] The individuals in our lives cannot be put into a recipe for a caring life and Voila!, we have a caring family.

I just wanted to make it clear that this book is not a recipe or formula for turning your kids into caring individuals or reshaping your family into a caring one. This book is a description of seven virtues that I have found through life and learning that can form the foundation of the caring family. It is in no way the exhaustive list of all the values needed but are the values that I have found to be essential ingredients, like great apples in the pie.

The last thing I want to share before jumping into the introduction is that I would caution you that this book is not intended to create guilt and shame. Dr. Kevin Lehman shares that "guilt is the propellent for most of the lousy decisions you have made as a parent."[3] This book was not written to create guilt or highlight that you have not gotten it right or things could have turned out differently for your family if you would have raised your kids or grandkids in a certain way. It is a book which aims to inspire us in the present and compel us toward a future where families are not sleepwalking through life, but are focusing on the role that the family plays in reshaping our world into a caring one.

INTRODUCTION

Imagine it is the early 1990s and you are in a twenty-five-member Christian college singing group from the Midwest, which is traveling around the United States performing at civic groups and churches. Your role in the group is to represent the college and at the same time share a message of hope, faith, and inspiration.

On this cold winter night, you ended up performing for a thriving church community located in a rural Western Maryland mountain town. This night's singing performance went very well, and those in attendance were particularly responsive to the message of encouragement and hope that you and the group have shared.

After finishing the evening performance, you are told that there are not many hotels in this small town, which is not at all a surprise to you. Your group leader shares that you and your friends will be hosted by different church members and will be staying in their homes.

You quickly recognize that this is going to be a luck-of-the-draw situation, and you are hoping for the best. A husband, wife, teenage boy, and younger girl come up to you and your friend and share that you will be staying with them. They are kind and look normal enough, which gives you hope that this will be a good night's rest.

You go home with the family who happens to live across the Potomac River in West Virginia, and everyone enjoys having a late dinner together. After dinner, the parents communicate that the teenage son and daughter have given up their rooms for the night so you and your friend can have privacy in your own rooms. The teenage son will be sleeping downstairs, and his sister will be in another room. You are tired from the travel and the long day, so you settle in for the night and quickly fall asleep.

All goes as planned until after midnight, when you are awakened by commotion in the hallway just outside your room and the sound of the rotary wall phone ringing. Are you dreaming? Unfortunately, you realize you are not dreaming and, with some trepidation, step out in the hallway to try to figure out what is going on. And this is what you see and the story you hear.

The teenage son is standing in the hallway in his shorts and t-shirt. His mom, who answered the ringing phone, is talking with someone you deduce is a neighbor. You look at those in the hallway trying to figure out exactly what is going on. You happen to look down and notice that the teenage boy has dirt and dried grass all over his feet and legs, an odd sight for the middle of the night in the dead of winter. As the mom is talking on the phone, you can hear the tone of the male neighbor's voice through the receiver, and he sounds upset and mad. But the mother is persuasive and is eventually able to calm him down and assure him that whatever they are talking about will never happen again.

The mother hangs up the phone, looks at her teenage son, and he begins to rattle off a far-fetched tale, a tale which will make you question how you ended up in this house and wonder how quickly morning will come. You have some interesting stories to tell from your travels around the United States, but this story from rural West Virginia is just unbelievable.

The son begins recounting his saga in a rapid pace and in a visibly shaken state. He shares that he was having a dream, and, in the dream, he had somehow ended up in someone else's house. In his mind, he could not figure out whose house he was in and how he had ended up in their basement. What he did know was that he needed to get back to his home and out of this strange one or this situation was not going to end well. He explains to those listening to him that he believes because he was sleeping in the basement for the night and was startled in his sleep by the furnace turning on, he became confused and disoriented and began to act out his dream.

He shares that he had this overwhelming sense of panic and needed to get back to his home as quickly as possible and out of the one he was in. He exited the sliding glass basement door and ran down through the field which was behind the houses in the neighborhood. He began searching for what his sleepwalking mind thought was his home. When he got to a house that he now thought was his, he checked all the doors, and they were all locked. There was no easy way to get back in, and this bad situation now was becoming more difficult and challenging to solve. He tried looking in the windows to see if his parents or his sister were awake and could let him back inside the house. But there were no lights on and he could not see his family.

In his dazed logic, he decided that he was going to need to pound on the front door and ring the doorbell to wake someone up to let him in. It was the middle of winter, and he was getting colder by the minute. He shares that he proceeded to pound on the door many times and rang the doorbell in rapid succession.

But even with all the pounding on the door and ringing of the doorbell, there was no response from inside.

The teenage son then voices that he determined that the only way he was going to get back inside what he thought was his home was to ram the front door with his body in an attempt to try to knock it down. After the third or fourth ramming of the door and the jarring of his head and body as it slammed up against the wooden front door, something changed about his perception of the situation.

The door he was ramming and slamming into suddenly did not look like the front door to his home. He then looked in the kitchen window, which was close to the front door, and noticed that the refrigerator was tan in color...the refrigerator at his house was not tan. It ...was...white. He then began to look for other things in the kitchen and noticed specifically that the kitchen sink was not in the same position as it was at his home.

As reality was setting in and as he was waking up, his stomach dropped, similar to when he is on the first drop on a roller coaster ride. He now realized that the house he was at was not his own. He had been trying to ram down the door of someone else's house!

He looked down and saw that all that he had on were his boxer shorts. He looked up and saw the stars in the sky. It was the middle of the night. The anxiety and sickening feeling continued to rise as it was now all becoming clear. He had been ringing the doorbell, knocking on the door, peering through the windows, and ramming the front door of his neighbor's house, not his. That was why his parents did not come to the door; they were not in that house!

As reality had then completely set in, he communicated that he took off running, again in a barefoot sprint, back down through the field and back to the house he had left. The sliding glass door was still open, and he quickly got back inside.

Breathing heavily and shivering from the cold, the young man sat back down on the couch where he had been sleeping. He closed his eyes and prayed that this was all just a very, very bad dream. There was no way he had left the house in a sleepwalking state and had done all the things he thinks he has done. The young man shares that he had almost convinced himself this was a bad dream until he looked down at his feet and legs which were caked in grass and dirt. Dirt and grass…from running through the field.

It was at this point that he came upstairs to share this unbelievable sleepwalking tale with his parents. And you had stepped out of the room you were sleeping in and happened to have a front row seat to this show. You ask yourself, maybe next time you will try to stay at the church or anywhere else other than with a family with a crazy sleepwalking son.

That sleepwalking son happened to be me.

Sleepwalking and Family Life

I have been a sleepwalker my whole life. It has ebbed and flowed, getting better for a season of time to only come roaring back when I am sick or stressed. It then levels off when I have recovered from the illness, or the stress has dissipated. And most of my sleepwalking stories are not nearly as interesting as the one I shared here, but I cannot count how many times I got up in the middle of the night in a heart-racing panic thinking I was late for school and rushed to the kitchen, poured my breakfast of champions, Fruity Pebbles, and began eating. I would eventually look up at the clock on the microwave and realize it was 2 AM, not 6 AM. It is probably all that 2 AM Fruity Pebbles sugar that has made my teeth so fragile.

Heather, my wife, could tell you countless stories from the early years of our marriage and how she endured my sleepwalking antics. There were times when I thought she was a patient whom I was responsible for at the hospital and times I thought there were snakes in our bedroom. The snakes we had seen on the show *Fear Factor* somehow ended up in my dreams. I would hide in the closet, wondering if I should wake Heather up to tell her there were snakes in the room or let her sleep. It is amazing she still loves me.

One of the interesting things about sleepwalking is that when you are acting out your dream, you have no idea it is not real. The scenarios I have lived out while sleepwalking could all be true and real. But they were not. They are things that somehow my mind is convinced are real, is hyper-focused on, and on which my mind is motivating me to act. These dreams compel some type of frantic action which is in mad pursuit of some life-sustaining outcome. I have never had a calm sleepwalking adventure. They are always anxiety-provoking, heart-racing, and mind-taxing experiences. When I wake up, I am exhausted . . . and embarrassed.

The sleepwalking stories are funny for others to hear about. And as I have shared them at parties or dinners, they are mostly embarrassing and, frankly, scary for me, as I am the one living them out. But I cannot help but make the connection between my sleepwalking adventures and larger cultural regression in caring and our families. Family members running anxiously, stressed and heart pounding, chasing something or some idea of life that is only really a dream or a figment of the current cultural imagination. All the while they are missing the opportunities to care for others and model and demonstrate what caring looks like to their children, setting an example that their children can follow.

Family members pursue, through the fog of the daily family routine, what they think is reality only to realize after being jarred by a death, loss of a job, crisis, empty nest, separation, children moving to university, divorce, or an unexpected diagnosis that what they thought was real and important about their family life, what they were frantically and hurriedly rushing toward, was neither reality nor priority. And then in moments of reflection, they recognize and regret the opportunities they had missed out on to care for others who had been going through similar circumstances like what they were experiencing themselves.

Maybe you are squirming a little and becoming defensive because your family has accomplished some things living in the hectic, frantic pace of life, only to be devastated that the results of your efforts were not what you thought they would be. Or maybe you have been embarrassed and scared, realizing that you have wasted precious time and energy with those you love the most, pursuing what Chip Ingram calls the 5 P's: Power, Position, Prestige, Productivity and Possessions.[4] And by pursuing them, you have missed the opportunities with your family to instill essential characteristics, virtues, and life values.

And as I look back, I am one of those parents who had younger children at home and chased after a lot of things including educational goals and degrees, work accomplishments, and adventures, and in the process missed out on some key windows of opportunity that I can never get back again, no matter how hard I try.

Similar to what Arthur Brooks shares, I am a father who wrongly chose being special over being emotionally present and happy, a father who did not know what Brooks also communicates that achievement makes you special, but love makes you happy.[5] I now realize that my kids were only three, five, or seven once. And

I cannot go back and change that as a father and husband, I was more of AAron than Ron.

AAron vs Ron

After finishing my first book, *A Caring Life,* I received a lot of feedback from readers on my comment in the dedication page about being both AAron and Ron. In the book, I dedicated the book to my family who loves me when I am AAron and when I am Ron. Many have wondered what I was getting at. Some figured it out, and some came up with some creative and interesting ideas. Maybe AAron really is a secret CIA agent?

The real story is that my kids were the ones that noticed a stark difference in their dad and came up with the AAron and Ron comparison. They both started pointing out that they liked Ron more than AAron. They liked Ron, the dad they had on vacation and who was less stressed, focused, and driven, the dad who was more present than AAron, who was always rapidly moving forward, serious, and stubbornly disciplined. Unfortunately, AAron was the one they experienced most of the time.

At first, I laughed and brushed it off, but the more I thought about it, I had to accept the reality that those closest to us know us best. And my kids had accurately realized that the type AA personality of AAron was not the same as Ron, who was available, present, and connected.

And that is one of the main reasons I am writing this book. As I reflect on my parenting, I wish I would have been more intentional about modeling a compassionate, caring father in the home. For sure, I cared for others and traveled the world to do so, and on occasion did get it right at home. My kids have confirmed that I was not abusive in any way, but I did fail numerous times to model an intentional, caring life within our family and to emphasize the virtues I knew to be true for a caring family.

Family and Caring

Family is often where caring is learned, ideas are formulated, connections are made, and where we begin testing and experimenting with caring for others. And I am more and more convinced that how our acts and concepts of caring are received and acknowledged in the family and in the home orients our trajectory for the future of each of our caring lives. Our family life, for better or worse, impacts how we see the world and those around us and our willingness to care for them.

As I considered those who I knew and had met over the last twenty-five years at the bedsides of those dying of cancer, those walking with grieving spouses and children at the loss of their wife and mother, and those that not only saw those in need of care but intentionally responded, a commonality I noticed was caring was valued, prioritized, and modeled in their family. And I cannot dismiss the impact of how one's family profoundly influences a caring life.

It is not to say that you had to grow or must grow up in a perfect family with no challenges or with parents that never made any mistakes. And I know that families can come in all different shapes, make ups, cultures, generations, and sizes. These differences impact us, but I do not think it is all of these factors that make the biggest difference.

I believe the biggest difference is what was modeled in our formative years when it came to caring for ourselves and others. Did those around us prioritize caring for others? How did my family prioritize being loyal to each other and to our friends and neighbors, to acknowledge the dignity we each have? Was my family emotionally honest, or did they hide their feelings or only express certain ones? Did your family model taking courageous steps to care for others? How was faith prioritized in your family? Were caring acts modeled, and how did your family view those to whom you showed compassion? What did you learn at home about being self-aware, others-aware, and culturally aware? Did your family prepare you to be resilient as you cared for others?

In the pages that follow, I would like to propose an intentional way of family life that centers around seven virtues that are essential for A Caring Family. Loyalty, Courage, Resiliency, Emotional Honesty, Spiritually Focused, Patience, and Transformational Awareness are the virtues that I wish I had more intentionally focused on while Heather and I were raising our kids. I would have valued someone sitting me down 20 years ago and having the discussion that I will share in this book. In a way, this is a book to my younger self, but unfortunately, I cannot relive or change the past. But the good thing is that you can benefit from the lessons I have learned the hard way.

How to Use This Book

Double U Moments

I consider myself to be a semi-intelligent person, an average student, hard worker, and middle-of-the-pack kind of guy. That was until I went to French language school. Then I thought I was a student that had somehow lost the pack at best and at times was not sure I was even in a pack. If you have ever tried learning another language, maybe you can relate.

One of those moments was when we were learning how to pronounce the alphabet in French. It was the basics of the language, but it was already a "swimming in the deep end of the pool" type of moment for me. In my Wiley Ford Primary School education, I never learned the international phonetic alphabet. I did not even know such a thing existed until I arrived in France. When I learned how to spell as a kid, the teacher told the class a word and how to spell it. No sounding it out. No questions asked. Just spell the word the way the teacher told you to. Memorize. That is how you learned to spell and got a good grade.

The teachers in the French language school I was attending were focused on the international phonetic alphabet, its wonderful characteristics, and how it could help us correctly pronounce words and the letters of the alphabet. Sarcasm noted. The focus on an international phonetic alphabet with symbols and squiggly lines only added confusion to my already spinning brain.

When we got to the letter W, my teacher explained that W was a very simple one to pronounce. It was simply double V with a French accent, of course. And everyone else in the class remarked how similar this was to the English pronunciation of W, as double U. In my twenty-seven years, it was the first time that I had ever made the connection, that W was a double U. This was apparent to everyone in my class. Except me. The guy representing West Virginia, proud and strong.

Some of the things I will share in this book will be like W moments for you. There may be W moments where you already know what I am sharing. It makes sense, and you have always known it and are modeling it in your home. And there will be other things that I will share and a light bulb will go off that something has been in front of you your whole life, and you had never seen it from this particular perspective.

A few important things to remember as you dive into the book:

1. This book is written for anyone who has a family and desires to grow in caring. Caring is not just for professionals. If so, we are in trouble. There are too many people in the world. If we leave caring to the professionals only, there is no way the tide will turn.

2. If you are looking for a book that teaches you how to raise the next great athlete, musician, or influencer, this is not the book for you. But if you are looking for a book that describes virtues that are vital in what truly matters and how we care for others, this is the book for you.

3. Please know that I have continued telling more stories in this book. As I suspected, I received a lot of feedback from readers of the first book on how the stories I shared kept them focused or helped refocus them on the subject at hand. And please know the stories are there for a purpose and reason, and I use stories and life experiences to highlight or further solidify the concepts I'm sharing.

4. As you read, you may quickly come to realize that I am a follower of Jesus. I am that unashamedly. How I care for people is deeply and richly shaped by His teachings and His commandments. You may not agree with me; I realize that. Please know that this book is not just for those who share my belief in Jesus. I do believe a family living like Jesus will be able to impact the world we live in by caring for those around them.

5. Consider laying aside the "Hitler scenarios" as you read. In my mind, Hitler scenarios are extreme cases. Do not let them hijack the essence of the book. If such a scenario comes to mind as you read, such as an abusive, unsafe family member, a family member who could hurt you emo-

tionally, physically, or in any other way, I recognize the concepts in this book do not apply. I consider those the outliers (five percent or less of people). This book is meant to speak to the other 95 percent of people and families, and not these outlier cases.

6. As I mentioned in *A Caring Life*, I am not a therapist or counselor, and for this book will add not a family specialist. I am a husband, father, son, brother, nurse practitioner, and missionary who is concerned about the direction our global culture is moving when it comes to caring for one another. I believe that the negative vitriol that pervades our airwaves, that is being played out from the state house to the schoolhouse, that is being experienced from the rural communities of West Virginia to the inner cities of California, and that our kids are being inundated with on social media is having a more profound impact than we can currently comprehend.

7. I am a learner and researcher at heart. I listen to twenty to twenty-five podcasts a week and read at least five or six books a month. It gets murky at times as I try to determine what are my original thoughts and what are thoughts I have learned from others. I have done my best to cite authors and sources throughout the book. If there are ideas or thoughts with missing citations, it is not intentional or me claiming someone else's work as my own.

8. This book is written in chapter format that will afford you the opportunity to process the concepts and topics by yourself or with others. Each chapter ends with a section entitled "A Caring Family." In these sections you will find practical questions that I have crafted to help you take steps on your caring journey. These questions take the

concepts in this book and help you think, pray, and process so that you can grow your caring family life.

9. If you are reading this book by yourself, I would encourage you to invite someone else along the journey. My friend, Roger, shares that self-evaluation is rarely accurate. Having someone else who knows you and someone you trust to ask you questions so that you can process them together will be invaluable.

Well, as I say in the introduction of *The Clarity Podcast*, "There is no better time than now to get started, so here we go!"

1 | LOYALTY
The Virtue That Provides Stability

What if I told you that there was a young mother in the prime of her life who was unexpectedly diagnosed with cancer, a cancer that would ultimately and precipitously take her young life, that her death would leave her husband without the love of his life and leave her two children without their mom, and that the circumstances that followed her untimely death would ultimately impact her family for generations to come and model to her children the loyalty of a father who tenaciously refused to give in and let his children be both motherless and fatherless? Would you be able to imagine it?

The story begins in the 1960s in rural America, where there was a young family with two children going about their everyday lives. James, the husband who had recently returned from serving as a medic in the Pacific theater during the Korean War, worked several different jobs to provide for his young family. His wife, Elma, loved being a homemaker with their young daughter and son. They were a lower middle-class family from varied backgrounds and experiences, but their young family and life together was good and looking very good for the future.

But one day, something inside Elma's body changed, a change that has happened to countless of millions and millions of people. A simple but deadly malfunction of the P53 gene. The P53 gene's job and responsibility is to control cell growth and to inhibit replication of abnormal cells with damaged or inaccurate DNA. Each day our body produces around 330 billion cells, and each time one of those 330 billion new cells is made, the P53 genes must verify that each new cell is an accurate copy of the original. If a cell is not an identical copy, the P53 gene causes the new, inaccurate cell to destruct or at minimum prevent it from replicating. Tragically, on that day in Elma's life the malfunction of the P53 gene let an error in cell replication take place and opened the door for a tumor to begin growing inside her body.

The insidious nature of cancer is that it is often undetectable in the early stages of its growth and development when it would be easier to treat. Frequently, cancer is detectable later on once it has developed a stronghold in one's body. And Elma's situation was no different. Days, weeks, and months passed as the tumor was undetectably growing inside her.

When she did start having symptoms, the tumor was already advanced and posed a significant challenge to treat. In the mid-twentieth century in rural America, those diagnosed with cancer did not have much trust and faith in the medical community's treatment of cancer. The twenty-first century's cancer treatment advances, like immunotherapy, high-powered scans, and advanced blood testing, did not yet exist. And the treatments that did exist were harsh and grueling as some continue to be today. The pain and agony of such treatments often turned human beings into physical and emotional shells of themselves, leaving the person with cancer weak, their families hurting, and both wondering how they would ever pay the enormous medical bills in the days and years to come.

The story of this young wife and mother did not unfold as her husband, kids, and family prayed it would. Her husband, James, did all he could and spent all he had trying to find a solution, a cure for his wife's cancer. Even with all his and the families' efforts, love for Elma, and their desire for her to live, the cancer eventually won out. My father says, "That cancer is a bully. And we are taught from a young age to stand up to bullies. When we stand up to a human bully it often goes away and looks for someone or something else to bully rather than pick on someone who is willing to stand up to them. But cancer is not a quintessential bully, because even if you stand up to it and fight, it often does not go away for long and if it does go away at all, it returns with a vengeance."

In the days and weeks after Elma's passing, the family was thrown into a tailspin as they had to face the reality that the wife and mother they loved was no longer living. As time passed, James received advice and counsel that he needed to begin to move on with his life. His young daughter was going to need a female in her life to teach her what it meant to be a woman. James was good-looking, hardworking, and charismatic, so finding another woman to be his wife would not be a challenge. However, most women who were looking to marry were not looking for a "package deal" that came with two young children to raise.

James was given counsel by friends and family, counsel that was common during this period in American history, which was that his two children could be taken in as second-class citizens with distant family members, or in a few years left to fend for themselves. And if he would choose one of these options, he would be able to move on with his life (I personally did not realize how common this was in mid-century America until reading the story *Boys in the Boat*. The early life of Joe Rantz, the main character in the book, is chronicled sharing that his mother died when he was 3 years of age. And ultimately, he was left to fend for himself following years of turmoil living with his father and stepmother.).[6]

But James refused to give his children up and made it clear that he was not going to be separated from them. They were a package deal. If a woman wanted to be his wife, his children would be with him, no hesitation, not up for debate or discussion.

And his young children were watching, observing, and learning about a virtue of a caring family—loyalty. Reggie Campbell shares, "Kids listen to what you say, but they watch what you do, and they remember the stories you tell."[1] James' children were watching their father model loyalty and write it into their family story, a loyalty that is defined by being devoted and faithful to someone or a belief even when it is not easy, fun, or without cost. Loyalty that is committing without any promises in return.

As James' grandson, my life's trajectory has been profoundly impacted by his decision to be loyal to my mom and my uncle, to stay when leaving was easier, to love when his heart was broken, and to provide when he was worn down from grief. He refused to allow the bond between himself and his children to be broken by life circumstances that were beyond his control.

His one decision of being loyal to his children changed their trajectory. His loyalty laid the foundation for his children to hear, see, and know that loyalty was a trait that their family would not just speak about and mention, but would live out. James provided an example to his children that they would then model to their children and generations to come.

What Are We Loyal To?

Loyalty is one of the values and virtues that our current culture seems to denigrate and dismiss as "old fashioned." The idea of being faithful and devoted to someone or some ideal seems to have fallen to the wayside. We have replaced loyalty with the "candy of the day" which is doing what you want for yourself: shunning devotion and faithfulness, doing what is best for you, being you, and everyone else will figure their lives out on their own.

The exception seems to be when we are using loyalty for monetization purposes or for our personal benefit. When I asked several people what first came to mind when they heard the word loyalty, all mentioned loyalty cards for stores, restaurants, airlines, etc. You name it, there is a loyalty program for it.

These programs are there to "reward" us for our loyalty for buying their products or spending money at their business. The reality is that these businesses are taking some of the money we give them in our transaction and returning a minute amount back to us as a "reward." And many times, the money they return is actually built into the cost of the product they are selling us.

Their business transaction with us somehow makes us feel that we have a relationship with them and convinces us to be loyal to them by returning for the "benefits" of the relationship. But simple economics would say loyalty programs are purely a business play or they would not be promoting it. Businesses must make money to survive. And the saddest part is they may be one of the reasons our definition of loyalty has changed.

Loyalty was never meant to be a transactional term, something based on what you do for me and what I get in return. My grandfather's loyalty to his kids was not a transaction. His loyalty was an inner motivation that required moral courage to be devoted to his children. In general, loyalty is being devoted to someone or to a belief without consideration of reward or benefit. Unfortunately, with our changing understanding of the word loyalty, it has become a transactional experience in a capitalistic world, rather than something that impacts the trajectories of lives and ripples throughout generations.

Foundations

As a kid, I loved going to church. I know some have had varying experiences in churches, but that was not my story. I never felt forced to go. I wanted to be there. Our family was there every Sunday morning and evening and Wednesday night. Each church meeting offered something that brought me a sense of community and connection.

Wednesday nights were Royal Rangers nights.[7] My Royal Rangers leaders taught me a lot about life. They showed me how to start a fire with one match and cook an egg. I learned how to tie rope knots and how to make fast racing pinewood derby cars. My leaders demonstrated how to upright a canoe in the water if it had overturned, how to use a knife, and how to sharpen an ax. We went on frostbite camping trips in the dead of winter to learn how to survive in the cold and what to do and not do if you were lost in the woods in the winter. But most importantly, they freely and wholeheartedly invested in my life and showed me the beauty of God and His creation.

The first camping trip I went on with the Royal Rangers was on the towpath along the Chesapeake & Ohio (C&O) canal. The towpath is the dirt or gravel path that runs 184.5 miles along the C&O canal and was where the mules who pulled the canal boats walked. The canal construction was started in 1828 and runs from Washington, DC, to Cumberland, Maryland. Although it was never the economic connector it was dreamt to be, it is by far one of my favorite places on earth to go for a run, jog, or walk.

Without adventure, there are few stories to tell, and my first camping trip provided lots of storytelling material. The Royal Ranger group began the trip by walking several miles on the towpath along the canal. We were carrying our camping equipment and supplies with us. If you have ever walked or hiked with your camping gear that you thought was necessary at home and then quickly began to wonder if all the gear was really necessary, you understand my thoughts that day on the canal.

After the long walk and some complaining, we arrived at the campsite. We goofed around for a while and then began looking for places to set up our tents. There were plenty of places to choose from, and I chose a spot in the shade.

I got all the poles and pegs out of the tent bag and began coming up with a plan. These were the days before the tent poles had the nice cord connecting the pieces that went together. So, I spread out the canvas part of the tent and resorted to reading the directions. I quickly realized I had chosen a bad place for the tent—a running theme in my life when it comes to picking places for tents.

What I did not see when I picked the spot for the tent and spread out the canvas part on the ground was the yellow jacket nest that I had covered with my tent. If you do not know much about yellow jackets, they are insects that belong to the wasp family and can be mean and aggressive. They can sting someone multiple times and will even chase you down if you have disturbed their nest.

As I started putting the poles in the tent, the yellow jackets quickly displayed their anger. I got stung more times than I could count and was ready to go home. Maybe this camping thing was not for me, but going home was not really an option.

My leader calmed me down, helped me choose a new place for my tent, and guided me on how to set it up. Since the other campers had already set up their tent, some of the older boys decided to go on a walk off the towpath through the brush and woods. They invited me to come along and supposedly were going to show me what it was like to be a true pioneer, chopping their way through the woods. I half-heartedly agreed to go with them for no other reason than to get away from the yellow jackets.

I remember one of them saying that real men do not take the path but make their own path. Making our own path randomly through the woods sounded more like something a group of teenage boys would do rather than a pioneer. And I quickly came to realize that the path was not a bad thing.

We made some progress hacking through the woods, but we had no idea how to get back. The zeal that got us going through the woods turned to panic. No one had any idea where we were or how to get back to the campsite. And for sure this was long before the days of cellphones.

But never fear, we were Royal Rangers. We had learned how to use a compass. So, several of us got our compasses out to plot our course back to the campsite. That would have worked well if we knew where the campsite was on the map. But we had no idea where the campsite was and realized when you are lost and panicked, your compass skills are not the best. After some prayers, some shed tears over the idea that we were all going to die in the woods and be eaten by bears, and some more prayers, our leader heard us screaming and came to our rescue.

And I do wonder if we are in a similar place culturally, where we have moved forward in a direction cutting our way to new ideas only to realize where we have ended up is not where we want to be. How do we make our way back to a place where loyalty is valued, not shunned and not just a marketing ploy?

Loyal to a Fault

The other night, my son, Josiah, and I were watching an episode of the Australian Survivor. At his age, it is one of the shows we like to watch together because it gives us insight into human interactions, strategy, and values. In the episode we were watching, one of the team members had to divide up food amongst tribe members. He got to choose what tribemate got what piece of food. Not a fun assignment, deciding what hungry people are going to eat. One of the things that made it harder was that the food items were not all equal in size or caloric value.

Josiah and I wondered what he would ultimately decide, if he would keep the biggest and highest caloric item for himself or give the best to others. In the end, the player chose to do what was best for the other members of the tribe and not what was superficially best for him. He ended up with a small piece of plain bread while others feasted on chocolate cake and other delicious items. One of the players made the remark that the tribe member who made the decisions was "loyal to a fault." In the context, I did not take it as a compliment, but rather as a sign of weakness and gullibility.

Before I go any further, I just want to be clear, I am not talking about being loyal to someone who is abusive emotionally, physically, or in any other way. I am not talking about being loyal to someone who is mistreating your devotion to them and causing you harm, or enabling someone as they harm themselves or others. And I am definitely not talking about toxic loyalty, as described by Scot McKnight and Laura Barringer in their book *A Church*

Called Tov, which covers over truth and promotes loyalty to the brand at all costs.[8]

The "loyal to a fault" comment led to some great father-son conversations about what being loyal to a fault looks like and whether it is a good or bad thing. We discussed how our world sees loyalty to someone else when it costs us something and how loyalty just does not seem to be considered a virtue worth striving for or a virtue worth acknowledging and affirming.

The questions I asked my son are the same ones I pose to you. What would our world look like if loyalty to a fault was being modeled and demonstrated in our families? And if loyalty is not being modeled and demonstrated in our homes, how will our kids and family members learn about its importance? How will they develop the care muscle to be and do for someone that offers nothing in return? My challenge for each of us is to model loyalty in our home.

As Josiah and I talked more about being loyal, I realized that loyalty was modeled when I was young in our home, and I believe it is one of the reasons that caring for those around me is so important to me. By modeling and demonstrating loyalty, my family gave me the mental and emotional space so that I could consider others. I never had to worry about who had my back or if my family would be there for me. And as we continued our conversation, I shared that just as loyalty was modeled in the home that I grew up in, I hoped that he knew I was loyal to him. My loyalty to him is not dependent on performance or being a mini-me, but that my loyalty to him is because he is my son and no other reason, just the fact that he is my son.

The Marine Award—That Almost Was Not

At the high school I attended, there was an award given each spring to one junior student. The award was called the Marine Award, and fitting to its name, a Marine would come to the school to present it. It was a pretty cool event. The considerations for the award were academics, athletics, comportment, and community involvement.

In the days leading up to the award presentation, the principal and vice principal notified me that I had been chosen as the recipient for my junior class. They advised me that it would be good to let my parents know so if they wanted to come for the presentation ceremony, they would have it marked off on their calendars. I let my parents know and my mom made plans to attend, but my dad could not get off work.

The day of the award ceremony arrived, and the principal came up to me during lunch and asked to speak with me. After lunch, I went to his office thinking we would be discussing the procedure for the award ceremony and what needed to happen. And I was surprised when he brought up another subject.

He began with a phrase that is now common to ESPN *30 for 30* documentaries, "What if I told you . . ." The principal said, "What if I told you there had been a break-in at the concession stand at the football field, and we believe you are the one who broke in and stole things?" I started laughing, thinking he was not serious, that maybe this was some type of practical joke or some set-up. And I was thinking, "I thought I was supposed to be getting an award in about two hours for my character, moral character, which would be the exact opposite of stealing?" He was not joking, and this was not a practical joke. The whole thing just did not make sense.

I want to clarify that I was not a perfect teenager by any stretch of the imagination. But breaking into the concession stand in broad daylight was not even in consideration. I started to nervously laugh, and the principal quickly reminded me that this was not a joking or funny matter. He continued by sharing that one of the janitors had seen me at lunch with chewing gum, and the janitor noticed that I had given several pieces of gum to those who were sitting around me. The janitor reported me because I had given chewing gum to my friends. Were they serious?

The principal asked if I wanted to go ahead and admit that I had broken into the concession stand since they had evidence that I was handing out gum. I told him that the gum I handed out was Carefree peppermint gum that my mom had bought for me, and not something you would buy at the concession stand. And by his reactions, I could see that he was not convinced that I was telling the truth.

He continued by telling me they had called the West Virginia (WV) State Police, and they would be coming to take fingerprints from the concession stand, and he wanted them to fingerprint me to see if I was a match. I just kept shaking my head. This made no sense at all, but if they wanted to take my fingerprints, have at it. I had nothing to hide.

As we waited for the WV State Police to arrive, the Marine who was there to present the award walked into the principal's office. After some quick greetings, the Marine asked who was going to receive the award and if he could meet the student beforehand. The principal proceeded to point at me, and then shared that I was under suspicion for a break-in, and he was not ready to move forward with publicly recognizing me until my name was cleared. Understandably, the Marine had a puzzled look on his face and looked back at me. I told him that there was no way I had broken into the concession stand and stolen stuff.

The next person through the door of the principal's office was my mom, who was coming to take pictures of me receiving the award. She walked into the principal's office looking for me, because my friends had told her that was where I could be found. So, it was now me, the principal, the Marine, and my mom.

My mom greeted everyone and asked how I was doing and if I was ready to receive the award. The principal interjected that he was not sure if I would be receiving the award that day or not, because I was considered to be the prime suspect for breaking into the concession stand. Of course, my mom wanted to know why I was a suspect, and he shared the whole story of the concession stand, me chewing gum, giving it to my friends, and being their focus in their investigation.

Family Messages

I recently interviewed Rick Langer on the book he co-authored with Joanne Jung, *The Call to Follow*.[9] The authors clearly show that we have an American culture focused on leadership and casting our own vision for life. Rick shared in the interview that maybe this has to do with Disney's portrayal of the ideal world, or maybe Disney knows what sells and people want to hear and gives it to them.

As I was preparing for the interview with Rick, I began to wonder if this increased concentration on leadership has to do with the idea that at a young age, we commonly encourage our children to not be followers. We encourage our kids to not follow the crowd, not to do what everyone else is doing, make your own decisions, and not to give in to peer pressure. Parents can communicate statements like "friends will want you to be loyal to them but may not be loyal to you when it is not beneficial to them." Maybe you never have said any of these things, but I know I have. And in the context of avoiding drugs, danger, promiscuity, violence, and unwise decision-making, I agree totally with this line of thinking.

But as a parent and for my family, I do not believe I clearly differentiated to my kids when following and being loyal were the virtuous and preferred choices rather than the undesirable ones. I failed to have those conversations. For sure, I did not have bad motives but was not intentional about explaining the difference between when following, supporting, caring, and being loyal were the right choices and when they were not.

These conversations about leading and following are ones I wish I would have had with my kids when they were younger. And I would encourage you to be intentional about having them with your kids and family members because being loyal and following and serving in the context of a caring family are just as important as conversations of leading and charting your own path. And I believe the place for these conversations are in the context of the family.

The Rest of the Story

You may be wondering how the rest of the story unfolded with me and the Marine Award. Once my mom heard the story, she looked at me and asked me if I had broken into the concession stand. I responded no, that I had not broken into that concession stand or any other, and that the gum I was chewing and that I had given to my friends was the gum she bought. She did not ask to see the pack of gum. She just needed to hear if I did it or not.

She turned to the principal and told him that I had not broken into the concession stand. And that I would not be fingerprinted until they had some real evidence that I was the one who did it.

Furthermore, she had come to see me receive the Marine Award and I would be receiving the award as planned. The principal and Marine both looked at her, looked at me, and looked at each other, and then we walked into the auditorium where I received the Marine Award. And by the way, they did catch the guys who broke into the concession stand, and amazingly it was not me or any of my friends.

Loyalty is a lesson we can speak about in our family, but it is ultimately best taught by modeling and demonstrating it in the family. Or as Scot McKnight shares, "We learn more by emulation and imitation than by information."[10] If we desire for our family to be a caring family, let's emulate and demonstrate that loyalty is paramount.

A Caring Family

The importance of the virtue of loyalty in a caring family cannot be overstated. Parents, grandparents, aunts, uncles, and other family members have the opportunity to model and demonstrate what true loyalty looks like. But families will need to push back against our current culture which has shifted the definition of the word loyalty from an inner motivation that is predicated on moral courage to more of a transactional term where loyalty is based upon a mutually beneficial situation. Families also need to model that loyalty does not mean walking away when the mutual benefit deteriorates or becomes inconvenient but stays and cares.

I would encourage you to have age-appropriate conversations in your family concerning loyalty, its expression in your family, how loyalty impacts caring, and what your family is loyal to. Please use these questions as possible starters.

Family Messages

1. What are some examples of loyalty in your family story?
2. How has loyalty impacted your family's trajectory?
3. Does your family model and demonstrate loyalty? In what ways?

Loyalty to a Fault

1. Have you ever used the phrase "loyal to a fault"? What did you mean by it?
2. Did you consider being "loyal to a fault" a good, bad, or indifferent thing?
3. Are there times that being "loyal to a fault" could be detrimental to a relationship and caring for someone?

What Are We Loyal To?

1. Who are some people in your life that you are loyal to?
2. Do you think loyalty is something society values? What are some reasons you feel this way?
3. Is it possible that marketing and business strategies have changed our definition of loyalty?

Foundations

1. How do you think loyalty impacts the ability and the desire to care for others?
2. Have you ever experienced loyalty in caring? How did it make you feel?
3. What are some ways you can use loyalty to model caring in your home?
4. What are some actions your family could take to model loyalty to others in their times of need?

2 | EMOTIONAL HONESTY
The Virtue That Provides Understanding

In the Summer of 2020, our family had planned to move to Kenya from Madagascar. By that time, we had lived in Madagascar for fourteen years and loved our time there. We had great friends, a strong community, and felt connected to the Malagasy whom we were there to serve. From caring for the kids at the orphanage to teaching at the Bible school, to caring for those who lived far from quality medical care, we were blessed to have lived and served those years of our life on the Big Red Island.

I am sure I am a bit of a revisionist in my history, forgetting a lot of the challenging times in favor of the good times, forgetting about living through coup d'états and outbreaks of the bubonic plague, measles, and dengue fever. Madagascar will always hold a special place in our hearts if for nothing else because that is where Heather and I raised our kids in their formative years and the place my kids refer to as Home.

Our move from Madagascar was spurred on by a change in our roles and responsibilities within the mission organization we serve in. In the spring of 2020, with many of the international borders closed due to COVID-19 (Covid), the option of moving directly to Kenya became more challenging and less and less likely. The house we were living in, and our belongings in it, had been packed up before we knew that Covid was truly going to be a worldwide pandemic. And I was one of the people who thought it would not end up stopping the world the way it did, but as the pandemic developed and the world slowed down, we had no way to leave the island.

In the midst of preparing to move, we made the decision to take our two Coton du Tulear dogs with us from Madagascar to Kenya to help us with the transition. We had heard several people share in the same breath about how it helped their family with their transition and at the same time was a huge headache to do the paperwork. We chose to focus on the value of taking them with us, and I began the tedious process of getting the required permits, the airline approvals, the vaccines, and their microchips. But all in all, it did give the family something to think about and focus on rather than Covid and the turmoil that was going on in the world.

With the stress of the delayed departure, the turmoil of Covid, and the challenges of getting the permits for the dogs, we needed something joyful to look at amid all our boxes. So, we put up our Christmas tree in June, and it stayed up until the moving trucks came in November. That old plastic tree was a daily reminder to us that we could choose joy, but it was also a physical sign of something I would learn more about in the coming days, my fear of being emotionally honest.

After waiting for what seemed longer than it really was, we finally made the decision to leave Madagascar on a repatriation flight to the United States (US). The route was not the most desirable or direct, but we could fly to the US, spend the holidays with family, and then depart from the US to Kenya. It was not an ideal plan, but we were ready to move on and this would work.

Despite the Covid restrictions, the trip back to the US was not too chaotic and the dogs did fine in the cabin with us on the long plane rides. I was frustrated that I had gathered all the documents for the dogs to travel with us, only for the resulting pile of paperwork and the trees sacrificed to make said paper to be in vain. Only one person during the whole trip to the US asked to see any of it. I could have been carrying lemurs or fossas for all they knew.

Once we quarantined in a hotel for a few days, we got to see family. We did enjoy being back in the US for the holidays, but like many other people during the winter of 2020, we became personally acquainted with Covid.

One of the good things about being in Madagascar during the pandemic was getting to follow the interesting rules when it came to Covid. One of my favorites was you had to always wear a face mask even if you were in a car by yourself. My wife and I had to physically distance ourselves in public even though we slept in the same bed at home. Another was the herbal tonic touted as the best treatment for Covid. I did not understand all the science behind the masking in a car, couples physical distancing, and the herbal tea. I do agree that it is unfair to criticize the past from the present, but all that to say, we made it to the United States without ever knowingly having gotten Covid.

My kids frequently poke fun at me about how I try to explain away symptoms of sickness. Probably the AAron coming out more than the Ron. Choosing the more Pollyanna view that something else could be causing the symptoms. And our first run-in with Covid was no different.

When the first member of the family had a headache and runny nose, I blamed it on living inside with the dry heat from the furnace. It was a stretch, but plausible. We did not have heaters in our home in Madagascar and living in an enclosed, dry-heated environment was not what we were used to. On the island, there was always fresh air moving in and out of our house because there were major gaps around the windows and doors. So, I convinced myself the heaters were the reason they were not feeling well.

When the next symptoms of cough and sore throat appeared, I explained those symptoms as caused by going in and out of the hot and cold, and shared that rapid temperature changes could be irritating to the respiratory tract. True. Unconvinced, my daughter looked me in the eyes, and said, "Come on, Dad! You are the professional here. You know these are all the symptoms of Covid. I think you need to start admitting that we are sick." She was right and the better doctor that day. They were sick.

After a trip to the local clinic and me losing my cool, a series of positive tests, and a trip to the emergency room where the staff greeted us in suits that reminded me of something out of the movie *Contagion*, I was left frustrated and discouraged. We tried to keep the sick people in our family together and the healthy people separated from the sick ones, but it was like an unending shell game.

Ultimately, I ended up in the basement of my parents' home . . . alone. I never did test positive but had the daily pleasure of receiving a call from a kind person at the Health Department making sure that I was continuing to quarantine. I must confess; I was quite irritated because those who had tested positive were once again free to move around after their quarantine ended. Even though I was healthy, I was still quarantined in the basement long after they were.

Once we were all out of quarantine, we made another very quick, well, quick for me, decision to try to go ahead with the move to Kenya, pending us all returning to health, being symptom free, getting our visas, changing our airline tickets, meeting the contact requirements to fly, and getting negative results on our COVID-19 tests. It was a lot of things to get in order in a short amount of time, but we wanted the kids to be able to start in-person class at their new school with the rest of the students. So, we did our best.

In faith that it was going to all come together, we had our Covid tests done and packed our bags. There was significant sadness in this move to Kenya as our dogs we had brought from Madagascar would not be making this trip with us. There were lots of difficult emotions, but as I learned in the coming days, I continued to try to focus on the positive, the bright side of the situation, such as the dogs would love life in America, Kenya was going to be great, and it was a great time to fly as there were very few people on the planes, so it would be like flying first class but paying economy prices.

Although we did not yet have our negative Covid results, our pastor friends from my home church, Doug and Pam, were kind enough to drive us to the airport. We spent the night and woke up the next morning with full, prayerful expectation that all the results would be negative. And they all were, except for one. Heather's test was still coming back positive. They told us that it could take up to three or four weeks for it to be negative. So, we made another quick decision, and we decided for me and the kids to go ahead and fly to Kenya and get them enrolled in school while Heather waited for a negative test result.

As the kids and I boarded an eerily near-empty plane, I continued to try to orient us away from the difficult emotions and feelings of sadness and anger toward happiness, joy, and the positive aspect of our current situation. But the reality was that our situation was not a joyful one. I was faking it, and I am sure my kids could sense it, but I was not capable or maybe more not willing to be emotionally honest with them. It was a hard season of life for all of us, but I was uncomfortable being emotionally honest with myself and my family and did not see how my dishonesty was impacting all of us.

Emotional Honesty

Emotional and honesty are words that I may use frequently but can be a challenge for me to use together. Not that I am trying to be dishonest or unemotional, but I frequently struggle with being uncomfortable or uneasy expressing my emotions and feelings. I do not know how they will be perceived and whether the person I am sharing my emotions and feelings with is safe to share with or not.

I also know that there have been times in the past when I have let my emotions and feelings boil over onto someone else. The last thing I want to do is hurt someone else. I have also found the timing on when to share my emotions and feelings to be like a moving target. Sometimes I have shared how I was feeling and immediately knew I had made the other person feel uncomfortable or uneasy, which in turn made me feel more uncomfortable and uneasy for both of us.

Dr. Nicholas Jenner shares that "emotional honesty is the glue that holds the four pillars of trust, honesty, respect and mutual benefit together. It allows us to be intimate, vulnerable and connect deeply with another person."[11] He continues on by writing that although it is of such great importance, we often avoid it at all costs. But what are some reasons that we would avoid a virtue that is so valuable?

I believe I avoided being emotionally honest with others because I was not being emotionally honest with myself. I dressed up my reasoning for not exploring why I was not emotionally honest with myself, but ultimately, I have concluded that it was out of fear of not knowing what it would require of me and the reality of the unknown of exploring how I truly felt.

What drove me to begin working toward emotional honesty was the realization that if I could not be emotionally honest with myself, I could not be emotionally honest with close friends and those I loved the most. And if I could not be emotionally honest, I was modeling for my kids that they could not be either, and it is difficult at best to have a caring family that cares for themselves and others if emotional honesty is not championed.

The saying that change comes when the pain of remaining the same is greater than the pain of changing defined my situation. And the pain of not wanting to live a life of not truly knowing others and not being truly known was greater than the pain of working on becoming emotionally honest.

Dr. Chip Dodd has helped me grow in my understanding of my feelings and emotions and helped me better identify when I am experiencing feelings and emotions so that I can be more emotionally honest. When Chip and I talked the first time, we discussed feelings and my description of them. I learned that I had a much broader vocabulary for my feelings. I was thinking it was because I was a West Virginian and we are known for waxing eloquently. But I quickly learned that this was not because I am so verbose or so poetic.

In his book, *Voice of the Heart*, Chip shares that we have eight primary feelings which are hurt, lonely, sad, anger, fear, shame, guilt and glad.[12] You can quickly see that there are seven of these feelings that some may consider negative or feelings to be avoided, and one to be pursued. Maybe you are healthier than I am and do not see your feelings this way. But unfortunately for me, this is how I had lived much of my life and what I was modeling in my family. Basically, pursue gladness, and if you experience any of the others, reorient quickly, and do your best to move back to gladness. And that approach to life limits our ability to care for others.

You may be thinking or pushing back on the idea that we only have eight feelings. And I was there pushing back just like you, maybe even harder, because I had built my life around my convictions on this and this rule of life of only wanting gladness.

I asked Chip about the feelings of being frustrated, irritated, expectation, and excitement. These are all feelings too. Right? As we talked, Chip pointed me back to something he wrote in his book, "When talking about feelings, any words that are not these eight are a step away from the truth, a step away from the pure experience of the heart's depth, and a step away from how God made us."[12] The more words and descriptors that I added, the less honest I was being with myself, others, and God. The reality was I was not using the words emotions, feelings, and honesty in the same sentence.

Created to Be Emotional Beings

If you would have asked me four or five years ago if I thought emotions were a good or bad thing and if being emotionally honest was paramount for a caring family, I would have probably resisted the idea. When someone was telling a story and would share that a person became "very emotional" or even "emotional," the mental picture that would have come to mind would have been of a person crying because they were angry or sad. For some reason, when I thought of someone being emotional, I did not think of them being joyful or glad. I had a negative slant toward emotions.

Maybe this negative slant came from the language I would use or heard being used to describe emotions. When I was growing up, whether it was an angry parent at a little league baseball game or someone at the store, I would hear people describe the situation as someone "losing their composure." Someone losing their calmness was something I perceived to be negative and to be avoided. I also heard people say that they were "overcome by their emotions." I did not want to be overcome by anything. And this further solidified in my mind that the best way to not be overcome by something was not to be around it and avoid it.

And because of these conclusions, I naively tried to navigate around emotional situations. I did not want to lose my composure and really did not want to be around someone else who was losing theirs because I did not like the instability that went with it. I did not want to be overcome by my emotions and was not excited when someone else was overcome by their emotions. Whether I was at school, at church, work, or in a team meeting, I was most content when there was peace and calm. And that is what I sought in life, peace and calm. No bumps in the road, just moving through life . . . fast, focused, happy, and steady.

If other people became emotional, I became uncomfortable, because I did not know what to do or how to act. Was I supposed to say something? Was I supposed to be quiet? What if I made it worse? What is the right thing to say?

Lessons from Sam

One of my favorite things about hosting *The Clarity Podcast* is that I get to interview remarkable people on subjects of which I have interest. I then get to grow from their wisdom and knowledge. When I interviewed Sam Farina for the podcast, he shared that our emotions and feelings were created by God for a reason and a purpose.[13] They were not something to be avoided and looked down upon. His reasoning was that if God had intentionally created us with feelings and emotions, then they were not something I should be trying to avoid in my life and the life of others.

Sam Farina shares that emotions are beneficial because they send signals. But emotions seemed to be a foreign language to me, and I was not able to adequately translate or interpret the signals emotions were sending. I was not adept at deciphering what my emotions or other people's emotions were communicating. All I knew was when someone started sharing their emotions, I would start to squirm in my seat. And, because of this, I was greatly limited in my ability to care for others, to care for myself, and to model emotional honesty with my family.

Sam explained that emotions were something to embrace and be thankful for. He continued by sharing that emotions and feelings were a God-given method of communication. I just had never thought of feelings and emotions in this way, but I knew that healthy relationships rise and fall on communication. And if I was able to begin to see emotions and feelings in this light, my relationships would be impacted in a positive way and I would be able to model emotional honesty to my family. Thank you, Sam.

A Sore Butt

When I was growing up, I wanted to play organized American football. I already played at school and in the field behind our house, but I wanted the uniform, mouth guard, shoulder pads, helmet, and the whole experience. I was also sure I was going to be the next John Riggins. (I know that dates me.) If you do not know who he is, just think of a big, powerful American football running back.

Much to my discouragement, my parents were not fans of organized football, and they did not want me playing on an organized team. When I would ask the question most kids ask when they do not hear what they want to hear, "Why?", the explanation I got always seemed to stem from an incident where one of my relatives got hurt playing football. From then on, it was decided that Santmyires do not play football on organized teams. It was just not worth the risk. People who played on teams got hurt. If I played on a team, I was going to get hurt.

However, I was a persistent and persuasive young man, and my parents relented and agreed to let me play one year and one year only. That one year was 8th grade for the Ridgeley Rams. For that year, I was a fullback and defensive end and really enjoyed playing. I loved everything about it. The uniform, pads, helmet, and mouth guard made me feel like a real player, and the tradition of wearing your game jersey to middle school on Fridays was icing on the cake.

But then, you guessed it, I got hurt. Just as my parents had warned me. In one of the games, I was blocking up the middle and the next thing I knew, someone rammed their facemask into my tailbone. Even today, thirty-three years later, if I think about it hard enough, I can vividly remember the pain shooting up my spine and throughout my body. As I lay on my side in the middle of that football field, I was in agony and full of emotions.

In the days that followed, my tailbone stayed progressively sore and tender to touch. Anytime something touched my tailbone whether that was a piece of clothing, a hard seat, or a cushioned seat for that matter, I was in pain. Whenever I sat down, I sat sideways to avoid anything touching my tailbone. I was truly a "pain in the butt" or "sore butt" kind of guy.

But I had one year to play football, and I did not want to miss half the season due to having a sore, cracked tailbone. So, one of my coaches devised a padding system made from refrigerator foam that I could wear under my uniform. It was big and thick and was not the trendiest thing to wear. It did protect my tailbone from anything touching it. I felt little to no pain if I wore this three-inch-thick cushion.

I finished playing the season wearing the thick padded cushion and scored a few touchdowns. But the sore tailbone lingered on and on. And as you may have guessed, I did not go on to football greatness or stardom. One year and one sore butt was enough for me.

As I think about my past perceptions of feelings and emotions, they were very similar to my sore tailbone. Emotions were something that if I would leave alone, they would not cause me any problems. It was when I touched them that they became noticeable and problematic. If I could fashion a padding system like the one for my tailbone so my feelings and emotions did not come in contact with anything or if they did were cushioned, I would be fine.

And I carried my awkward uncomfortableness with feelings and emotions into our marriage, family, and parenting. It is one of the many things I would go back and do differently. As I mentioned earlier, we cannot change the past, and I know that. But if I could go back and do that season of life differently, I would focus on creating a safe space in our home for each member of the family to experience the full range of emotions and feelings, without me trying to dismiss, minimize, fix, or reorient how they were feeling. I would have not championed irrational behavior and weaponization of emotions and feelings but would have created a safe space for us all. And I am so grateful for my kids sharing how this impacted them.

Coming to Light

For the most part, the transition to Kenya was not a smooth one for me. I had somehow convinced myself that I had transitioned from the United States to France, France to Burkina Faso, Burkina Faso to the United States, and the United States to Madagascar, so the transition to Kenya should be easy. My thinking was that by now, I should be a professional at doing international moves and the cultural transition that goes with it.

My kids and wife are professionals at transitioning and international moves, and I am a very distant fourth. My kids have been in and out of different schools. They have experienced different teaching systems and been forced to learn in multiple different languages and under different cultural pretexts. Heather has had many of the same life experiences as our kids, so she has helped them process the emotions as we have transitioned from one place to another. Ulrika Ernvik communicates that children of global nomads have no real choice but to quickly figure things out in a new environment as they are frequently not given a choice to go to school or not.[14] All the while their parents return to a safe environment of their choosing. Like I said, my kids and wife are way better than me.

Once we had all arrived in Kenya, our family went through a debriefing process that involved activities and counseling sessions. Heather and I lead member care in Africa for the organization we serve in, and our kids often feel like the guinea pigs as we look for resources and opportunities to recommend to others. We believe that going through resources before recommending them to others is best practice. So, my kids might be partially right that they are guinea pigs.

I had interviewed Lauren Wells on her work with Third Culture Kids and the power of unstacking your grief tower.[15] Lauren's basic idea is that as we go through life we continually are adding to our tower of blocks, aka grief tower. If we can intentionally take the blocks off the grief tower and process them, there is less of a possibility that the tower will come crumbling down. And if it does come crumbling down, processing the pieces of our grief tower at regular intervals helps prevent the added weight of trying to process all the blocks at one time, which can be overwhelming and exhausting.

With our move from Madagascar, the COVID-19 experience, and the looming transition of our daughter going to university, Heather and I knew we had quite a few blocks on our family's tower and wanted to do something intentional to address it. The debriefing was a valuable and transformative time for our family as we considered the past, reflected on our current circumstances, and dreamed about the future. I would recommend it for any family going through transition.

One of the major takeaways from our debriefing weekend was that in our home, I did not provide a safe space for my kids to be angry or sad. They shared that whenever they were sad or angry about something, I was quick to give another perspective or dismiss how they felt rather than being willing to listen and hear them. They felt that I often pushed back on what they were sharing if it was not joyful, happy, or glad.

Sadly, what they shared during the debriefing time was 100 percent true and our recent transition was example number 1,004. I thought my job as the dad was to help them move away from difficult emotions, and by rapidly doing so I did not acknowledge their feelings and emotions and did not listen to them. If I would have just known the proper response to their emotions which I have learned from Ted Lowe, such as "that is understandable" and "tell me more," I believe I could have created a more emotionally safe place in our home.

Ted Lowe shares in his book, *Us in Mind*, about how we can caringly respond to others' emotions and feelings.[16] The subject of his book is marriage, and I have found the wisdom he shares to be equally applicable to most relationships in my life. Ted communicates that when someone shares a story, we often want to solve the problem, propose a different view of reality, share our own experiences, or help reshape the event. And he shares one of the most powerful answers we can provide when someone shares their feelings and emotions with us is to say "that is understandable."[16] That is it. No need to come up with a deeply theological or existential thought. No need for a pithy quote or proverb. By sharing "that is understandable," we are acknowledging and letting the person know that they belong, matter, and are known.

I wrote more extensively about belonging, mattering, and being known in my first book, *A Caring Life*, and how when we care for someone, we demonstrate these three things. Belonging, mattering, and being known are vital for human connection and for communicating dignity and value. I believe that unless we can model what it means to be emotionally honest in our families and create a safe place for emotions to be shared, our family members will most likely not be able to be emotionally honest with themselves and others, and this will impact their ability and desire to care for others.

A Hypothesis

As I did research for this book, I had a hypothesis that went something like this: that when families provide a safe environment to recognize, express, and process emotions and feelings, those in that family are more likely to make decisions to care for others.

The inverse would be that when families do not provide a safe environment to recognize, express, and process emotions and feelings, those family members would be less likely to care for others. Basically, a family's ability to provide a safe environment to recognize, express, and process our emotions and feelings impacts our empathy for others and our moral and ethical decision-making.

I was basing this hypothesis on the understanding that when we are in unsafe environments, the part of our brain that makes executive decisions turns off. We move into flight, fright, or freeze state. And if family members are constantly concerned for their emotional safety when they express their feelings and emotions, I would think it would impact their decision-making when it comes to caring for others.

As with most of my hypotheses, someone else smarter than me has already thought about it, researched it, and published a book about it. I am rapidly realizing original thought is hard to come by. In her book, *Emotional Agility*, Susan David shares that when parents provide a home where children can experience the full range of emotions in a safe environment, they learn three key things:

1. *Emotions pass. They are transient. There is nothing in the mental experience that demands a response.*
2. *Emotions are not scary. No matter how big or bad a particular feeling seems in the moment, I am bigger than it is.*
3. *Emotions are teachers. They contain information that can help me figure out what matters to me and to others.*[17]

David continued by sharing that when parents model an empathetic response to their children's emotions and feelings, it provides an example for them to do the same for others.

Once again, I am not saying that family members should allow emotions or feelings to be weaponized, controlling, or used to cause destruction. But for kids to be able to express their emotions and feelings, parents must become comfortable with their own emotions and feelings. If we desire for our family to be a caring family and for our kids to be caring toward others, how we respond to their emotions and feelings impacts their future actions.

Emotions, Feelings, and Mood

As I continued my deep dive into how caring families are emotionally honest, where emotions and feelings are not dismissed or discounted, I thought it would be good to try to nail down clear definitions of emotions, feelings, and mood. This is another area that if I could go back and change how I raised my kids up until this point, I would have had family-agreed-upon definitions of feelings, emotions, and mood. I believe by having definitions it would have provided clarity and boundaries, and with boundaries and clarity there is safety.

In my everyday life and work, I hear the word feelings, emotions, and mood being used interchangeably, and I know I have used them just the same. As I began looking for definitions for these words, I found out I was not the only one who was somewhat confused on what was what. I also found that some people feel very passionately one way or another, and some feel comfortable using feelings, emotions, and mood interchangeably. Ultimately, variations in the definitions and descriptions of these words exist, and different nuances of these words are used by professional psychologists, counselors, teachers, parents, and guys like me.

Could this lack of clarity in the similarities and differences in feelings, emotions, and mood be part of the origin of the problem and tension of families not being able to express their emotions and feelings? Maybe we are using words that have different definitions and meanings. Seemingly thinking we are communicating, we may be causing more confusion than help. Or maybe this is one reason why we fail to do what Toni Nieuwhof encourages us to do in using emotions and feelings as signals and not focusing on them but rather the expectations behind them. [18]

In the research looking for definitions, I discovered the Human Affectome project whose focus is affective neuroscience.[19] I am not going to geek out on you here, so please stay with me. This multinational and multidisciplinary team was tasked to find a comprehensive and functional model for emotions and feelings and to address the debate of emotions as natural kinds.

The vast group of researchers realized that there was much ambiguity and inconsistency surrounding the terms emotions, feelings, affect, and mood and the ambiguity and inconsistency made it hard to study them and compare research done by different individuals and groups. And for scientists to move forward together in their research, there would need to be agreed-upon definitions so that they were discussing, comparing, and researching with the same foundational definitions in mind. They realized the definitions of emotions, feelings, and affect would be vitally important.

The team presented great definitions and descriptions written for scientists, not for children or use in the family setting. I needed a dictionary and the "phone a few friends" option to help me interpret them and to finally come up with something I think would be applicable for most families. Here are the descriptors I have found that help me better understand the similarities and differences.

Emotions: *immediate, intense, objective, and temporary responses to stressors from the outside world. These are physiological responses that we have little control over, but we do have control how we respond to them. They originate from the inner part of the brain that is not adept at logic.*

Feelings: *delayed, less intense, subjective, longer lasting, and mentally processed concepts that provide understanding to emotions. Feelings are influenced by our past experiences, opinions, and beliefs, and originate from the logical part of our brain.*

Mood: *delayed, prolonged, generalized, and the descriptor of overall state of being. Mood shows momentum. Mood does not pertain to any one stressor but is reflective of the cumulative impact of multiple things taken and interpreted as a whole.*

The Ten-Minute Practice

As I have shared, one of my real concerns as a parent was that if my kids were feeling angry, sad, frustrated, or discouraged, they would get stuck there and ruminate on these feelings and emotions. I feared they would rehearse and replay them and that they would not be able to move through these emotions and feelings that I had labeled negative. And as a result, I was concerned that they would end up being limited by anxiety or depression and spiral downward. Some may think that my concern was illogical, and I respect that. However, it was a real, palpable concern for me.

In our world today, it is hard for parents not to see, hear, or read about the increasing rates of anxiety and depression in our society. So, my concern for my kids and family seemed to be confirmed in the world around me in the books I read, shows I watched, conversations I engaged in, and stories that were told. I know confirmation bias can be a dangerous thing, but I could not shake it.

Although I wanted to do my best as a parent to help give my kids skills to move through their emotions and feelings, my approach of hurrying them through those emotions and feelings was misguided and ineffective. I gave my family little time, if any, to share and express their feelings and emotions before I wanted to pivot to helping them process their feelings and emotions so they could quickly forget about them and move forward.

Maybe you are a parent that has similar concerns as I did about your family and anxiety and depression. And at the same time you want your family members to have a safe place to express their feelings and emotions so that they do not feel dismissed. We just want a home where emotional honesty is valued so we can care for those in and outside our family unit. What is one to do?

One possibility that I could have exercised in our family when our kids were younger was what I started calling the ten-minute discipline. Nathan and Beth Davis share about the impact of rumination and how replaying negative experiences with friends over and over can be unhealthy.[20] They communicate that prolonged negative mental rumination always causes depression. The Davises share that setting an agreed-upon time limit when talking with friends gives the negative conversation boundaries and helps hold each person in the conversation accountable. I have found this to be so valuable in other areas of my life and exercised it, but for some reason did not consider putting it into play at home.

For sure, the discipline is not hard and fast and does have flexibility in it. I am not suggesting getting a stopwatch out or timer and placing your kids "on the clock." When someone is looking at their watch while you are sharing your feelings with them, it sends the opposite message of a caring one. Parents and family members will also need to be sensitive to each other and empathetic, and I believe having an age-appropriate conversation about this idea in advance and agreeing upon a general amount of time would be invaluable. Some people are faster processors and some are slower, and that should also be factored into the decision.

I think I would ask a question like, "I want our family to be a safe place to share emotions and feelings, and also want to walk with you as you move through these emotions and feelings. How would you feel about the idea of putting a boundary on the amount of time that we share negative experiences so that we can help each other process, see a different perspective, and begin moving forward? And if there is ever a time that we need more time than we agree upon, all we have to do is ask each other."

You know your family and children and can come up with an amount of time you believe to be healthy for all involved. I do think having a set amount of time gives space for someone to share their feelings and emotions and can help us move forward together. Some have pushed back on this idea of the ten-minute discipline, and some have asked if I had a time limit on being joyful and happy. These are great questions.

My response is that if we want to have a caring family that in turn cares for others, then moving through feelings of anger, sadness, frustration, and discouragement are paramount. I have met many people who find strength to care in joy, but have met very few, if any, who find strength to care in anger, sadness, frustration, irritation, depression, or anxiety. So, I am all for joy in our world and do not have a time limit on being joyful or happy. And I definitely am not suggesting limiting it.

A Caring Family

Emotional honesty is the virtue that provides understanding. God created us with emotions and feelings as ways of sending signals and communicating to ourselves and others. But oftentimes, our lack of a clear understanding of what emotions and feelings are can leave us wondering how to understand what they are communicating to us and others.

Add to this a feeling of being uncomfortable with feelings of hurt, lonely, sad, anger, fear, shame, and guilt, we can drift toward not wanting to care for others experiencing these feelings. Families that provide a safe space for each other to share, in a respectful and loving way, their emotions and feelings help build a solid foundation for caring for others.

The importance of a home that is emotionally honest cannot be understated. I would encourage you to consider these questions yourself and then to discuss them in an age-appropriate way with your family.

Emotional Honesty

1. Did you grow up in an emotionally honest home?
2. How did that impact how you respond to your emotions? The emotions of others?
3. Who do you know that models emotional safety and emotional honesty?

Created to Be Emotional Beings

1. Do you consider emotions to be positive, negative, or indifferent?

2. How does an understanding that God created us with emotions impact how you perceive your emotions and the emotions of others?
3. Are you comfortable showing your emotions or do you feel you need to hide them?

Lessons from Sam

1. How do emotions send you signals and how can this help you be more aware?
2. What are some ways emotions communicate?
3. Do you agree that communication is vital for healthy relationships? How can emotions and feelings help you better communicate?

Coming to Light

1. As a parent do you provide a safe place for feelings and emotions to be expressed?
2. Does your family have an agreed-upon understanding of feelings, emotions, and moods?
3. What would each family member say it is like being on the other side of you?

Emotions, Feelings, and Mood

1. How do you define emotions, feelings, and mood?
2. Do you agree or disagree with the descriptors for emotions, feelings, and mood that were presented in this chapter?
3. What are some ways different understandings of these words could impact family relationships and desire to care for one another?

The Ten-Minute Practice

1. Do you think there is value in having something like the ten-minute discipline?
2. How can we have a discipline like this without making it legalistic?
3. Would something like the ten-minute discipline work in your home?

3 | COURAGE
The Virtue That Provides Strength

Before we moved our family to Madagascar, I had the opportunity to visit the island, check out the housing and schooling, and meet the team and church leaders. During that visit my host and eventual boss, Manuel, took me to one of the local French schools and remarked that it would be a great school for our kids. My first thought was that there was no way I was sending my kids to this school. Let's just say the curb appeal was lacking, and my expectations at that time were unrealistic. But like many things I have said I would not do, we ended up sending both our kids to that exact same school. Manuel was right. It was a great school. Our kids received a first-class education, and we enjoyed being part of the school, its community, and the French cultural events.

One school event that still sticks out in my mind was Carnaval. Where I grew up in West Virginia, we had the usual school holiday celebrations such as Halloween, Thanksgiving, Christmas, Presidents' Day, Saint Patrick's Day, and several others. I had never been to New Orleans and had little exposure to the Mardi Gras scene. So, when my kids came home from school talking about

Carnaval, I had no idea what it entailed or what it was about. But it sounded like the word "carnival" to me, and carnivals can be fun, so that was my mindset going into the weeks leading up to the celebration at school.

During those early years, we carpooled with other families to take our kids to and from school. Carnaval created some great conversation points as our kids and their friends talked about the preparations for the event and their excitement and anticipation for us to see their work on the papier mâché Monsieur Carnaval. And my anticipation was building the more I heard the kids talk about it. It sounded fun and exciting, and I have found that the joy and excitement in the hearts and minds of your children is contagious.

The conversations about Monsieur Carnaval, the papier mâché man, did not stop once we got out of the car. Most evenings at dinner, our kids talked about how their classes were working hard on and being creative with the design of Monsieur Carnaval. Obviously, I must have not been paying much attention and was still thinking that this was a carnival with circus games, clowns, and rides. For that reason, I had it in mind that these papier mâché men were ten- to twelve-inch figures that the kids were making with their classmates for use as decorations or for use in one of the games.

The big day finally arrived for the Carnaval celebration at school. When we arrived, we were told it would take place at a center meeting area near the playground. It went as most elementary school events go with the 250 or so students all walking from their classrooms in single file lines following their respective teachers and forming into groups according to their grade level.

The principal greeted the parents and those in attendance and welcomed us all to the celebration of Carnaval. He was a great guy, and we appreciated his kindness to our kids and other non-French students. But as most parents do at these events, we were not paying much attention to what the principal was saying because we were all angling for the best place to take pictures of our kids. Several minutes into his presentation, I realized this was going to be unlike any school event I had ever been to. I was not in Wiley Ford anymore.

One of the first things that struck me was that Monsieur Carnaval was not ten to twelve inches tall but was more like ten feet tall. He was a massive papier mâché man. It was all becoming clearer to me now, and I understood that the kids were all working on different parts of him, not making ten- to twelve-inch individual men. Needless to say, I was way off in my estimation of his size and what they had been creating.

The next thing that made me pause was that several of the children were dressed in white costumes and were wearing white pointy hats. I had only ever seen these types of white outfits worn on television or in films. And it was never a positive or uplifting thing. It was more a look that brought terror to others, and not something this American expected to see at an elementary school event.

The presentation continued as Monsieur Carnaval was placed in the center of the school yard on what appeared to be a giant wooden cross. The design of the wooden structure may just have been the practical configuration that could hold such a large art project in a vertical position. But it sure did look like a papier mâché man on a cross. The children all excitedly gathered around Monsieur Carnaval and admired their work and at the same time kept a safe distance.

The teacher who was now leading the festivities proceeded to explain that Monsieur Carnaval was responsible for all the wrongdoing during the year. She continued by sharing that the children would have the opportunity to write their sins on pieces of paper and then throw those pieces of paper at Monsieur Carnaval because he was responsible for them. I am a slow learner, but it was at this point that I was really becoming perplexed. I was hoping that maybe my French was off.

When I was learning French, I frequently got the word for sin, *péché*, and the word for fishing, *pêche*, confused. I remember one time thinking I was asking the pastor of the church we attended if he was an avid fisherman. He responded that he was not. I insisted and reiterated again that I had heard that he was an avid fisherman. He responded again that he surely was not. Someone kindly nudged me and told me I was not asking if he was a fisherman, but I was asking him if he was an avid sinner. Was I confusing the words again today for fishing and sin?

But writing your fishing down on a piece of paper and throwing them at Monsieur Carnaval made little to no sense. I checked with one of our friends beside me and he shared that, yes, I was correct. She was asking them to write their sins down and was not asking them to write their fishing down. Although I was disturbed by the events, I was at least making some French language progress.

And some of the kids did just as the teacher instructed them to do and wrote things down on pieces of paper. They then balled the paper up and threw the paper at the feet of the Monsieur Carnaval. At this point, I was ready for the party to be over. But the excitement, amazement, or bewilderment had only just begun, and not for the better.

The teacher then explained that the children would get to vote by way of cheering whether they wanted Monsieur Carnaval to be burned up for his actions or to be pardoned to be put in storage for another day. I could not believe my eyes or believe what I was hearing. As the cheer voting began, it was very much in clear favor of sacrificing or burning Monsieur Carnaval. I kept thinking that there was no way that they were going to burn him.

However, with the clear vote against Monsieur Carnaval and his fate sealed, the school children were moved back and away from him and someone then lit him on fire. We all watched as he burned up in front of our eyes. I was speechless and could not believe what I was seeing. Some of the children cheered as he was burning up, and others were visibly disturbed by what was taking place.

The question for our family was how we would respond to this celebration.

Natural Courage

Growing up, there were many words that could be used to describe me, but courageous was not one of them. For instance, I always wanted to be the first to go to sleep at night, so that if someone broke into our house, I would not be awake when it happened. Somehow in my young mind, sleeping through a robbery was better than being awake for it. And to that end, I would frequently go to bed fifteen minutes before the end of the last television show that I would be watching with my parents and sisters, so that I could get a head start on falling asleep before they did—not real courageous.

Another example of my cowardness was when I played church league basketball as a young kid. Our practices took place in the gym of a mental health facility. The 250 feet between the front door of the mental health facility and the door of the gym were some of the scariest 250 feet I would ever tread. It felt terribly unsafe.

Sometimes I would run to the gym door hoping the mental health patients, whom I was very much afraid of, would not be able to catch me. (No one ever chased me.) I then went through a time thinking if I walked slowly, they would not notice me, that I would somehow blend in. (Many noticed and would make comments.) Either way, I was scared. And I could give you countless other stories from growing up that would illustrate my cowardice or lack of courage. Courage just did not come naturally to me.

The Tension

Reggie Campbell shares that the absence of fear is not courage, but courage is moving through fear and doing something despite it.[1] And although I was skittish and fearful, I did have a tender and compassionate heart.

I wanted to be able to care for others, but the challenge for me was that caring for others took a tremendous amount of courage, something I did not have. The tension inside of me of wanting to care for others and show compassion would often lose out to the fear that spoke louder and pushed harder. The fear that I surrendered to caused me to sit down when I should have stood up and led me to take the path of least resistance, not the path that required pushing through my fear with courage.

Whether it was standing up for someone who was hurting because they were being bullied, recognizing when someone new felt like they did not fit in at youth group and did not have a place to sit, or listening to someone as they shared about how their homelife was unstable and unsafe, it took courage to engage and act. But inaction was so much easier, took little to no courage, and did not require me to push through my fears.

As I have thought more about this, I am more and more convinced that the reason I did not have the courage to act and care was because I was unsure of the outcome and could not see how my actions would play out and how someone would respond. Would the person be receptive to my care? Would they push me away and then I would feel less than and embarrassed? What if

I was reading the situation wrong and they did not feel bullied? What if the bully started bullying me? How would the friends I wanted to keep in my life respond to me caring for someone else? The feeling of fear was somehow winning out. Fear and the path of least resistance were the known. The feeling of caring for someone and the courage it took to push through my fears were the unknown, and I did not have confidence to step into the unknown. And not stepping into the unknown created regrets in me and robbed others of acts of kindness and dignity that would have reemphasized that they belonged, they mattered, and that they were known.

Foresight

Foresight is the ability to predict what is coming based on what is occurring in the present and what has happened in the past. Or as Dr. Henry Cloud shares, the best predictor of the future is the past.[21] When it comes to caring, foresight is something that families can foster and grow by providing opportunities for their children and family members to experience what caring will do and how it will impact the caregiver and care receiver. Giving our families opportunities to muster the courage and push through the awkwardness and apprehension to see what it feels and looks like on the other side of fear is an invaluable gift, to see what caring feels like and the joys that come with it.

It also gives families opportunities to process and share what it looks and feels like when you gather the courage to push through and care for someone and it does not go as planned. It gives opportunities to experience how to bounce back when caring is not received, how to not take it personally when an act of caring creates problems and challenges for the caregiver, and how to remain resilient when it would be easier to quit, and how to push through fear and not build walls that would prevent us from caring.

I am thankful that my parents had the foresight and insight to recognize that my fear was holding me back, and if caring for others was part of our family's DNA, I needed to be able to push through my fears. My parents and sisters modeled and demonstrated to me what it was like to push through fear and get to the other side. They modeled this at home, work, church, and school.

My family gave me opportunities to care for others alongside them. When my courage was lacking, they lent me some of their courage so I could push through my fears and hesitations. I got to experience caring with my family members. And that is my challenge for each of us: to give our families opportunities to push through the fear and care . . . together.

Did our family always get it right 100 percent of the time? For sure, we did not. We did get to experience the heartache that comes from not getting it right, but we did not let the heartache create a bitter, jaded heart. We got to know the joys and challenges of when caring was well received and when it was not. And one of the greatest gifts my family gave me was letting me progressively in on what the truth of caring was and not some inflated or unrealistic ideal. My family showed me it is not some made-up fairy tale land, and they gave me the skills to adapt and bend but not break.

Realities

One of the most memorable events of my growing up years was going every summer to Potomac Camp for kid's camp. It was often the highlight of my summer. I loved the sporting events during the day. I loved the challenge of trying to find, in no less than six seconds, a girlfriend for the week who I would go to the Thursday night banquet with, only to sit awkwardly with her because I was no ten-year-old Casanova. I also loved going to the snack bar after church service which made me feel grown up and mature. And probably the thing I loved the most about kid's camp was it was a place where loving Jesus and following Him were encouraged, modeled, focused on, and emphasized.

There were some things about camp I did not like. My friends, Brandon and Seth, and I were often too few in number to be put in a room by ourselves. So, we often ended up sharing a room with five or six other young guys from another church. They would outnumber us which created interesting dynamics for being on the bottom of the proverbial totem pole. It is amazing the power dynamics amongst ten- and eleven-year-old boys and how young boys could stretch the truth more ways than a piece of chewing gum stuck on the bottom of your shoe.

I distinctly remember one year and two of the boys we were rooming with talking about their dads. One of the boys began talking about how big and strong his dad was. According to him, the buttons on his dad's dress shirt would frequently pop off due to his muscles flexing when he raised his hands in church. The same thing with his sport coats, he often ripped holes in them simply by shaking someone's hand. He shared how his dad once needed to move their car, and instead of starting it up and doing it the conventional way, his dad was able to pick the back end of the car off the ground and pivot it out of the way. I was thinking that this boy's dad must put Hulk Hogan to shame.

His friend began to share that his dad was not as strong as his friend's dad, but his dad was unbelievably fast. His dad was so fast that he could chase down bees as they were flying and catch them in mid-air with his bare hands. He shared that his dad would often run to church because it was faster for him to run than to ride or drive a car. And Carl Lewis had nothing on his dad. His dad could have won the Olympics, but just had too many other things going on to dedicate time to running in races.

I just kept thinking how lucky I was that I was getting to share a room with the sons of some of the strongest and fastest men in the world. How did I get so lucky? And the best part was that their dads were coming to pick them up at the end of the week. I would like to tell you I did not think much about meeting these men, but I could not wait until Friday to meet them.

Friday did finally come. And I was excited. The dads arrived but they were not the Hulk Hogan and the Carl Lewis I was expecting. The dad who was supposed to be the guy who moved cars by picking them up was struggling carrying his son's suitcase from the room to the church van. The dad who was supposedly faster than Carl Lewis and could chase down bees, well, he was winded just walking up and down the short hill near the building we were staying in. You can obviously guess that I was highly disappointed and recognized I had been lied to and was gullible enough to believe their stories.

Parents, grandparents, and family members, I am not suggesting lying about the realities of caring. I am not suggesting making it out to be something it is not. What I am suggesting is giving your children the opportunity to walk beside you as you care for others.

Overcomers

Stephen Blandino is a pastor, author, podcast host, and friend I have learned so much from. I highlighted his decision-making model in my first book and how it has helped me decide how to choose for whom I should care. As I was writing this chapter, I interviewed Stephen about his article, Overcoming Leadership Fears.[22] I believe that the ten fears that he lists are some of the most common that we encounter when caring for others. And having multiple, short, intentional conversations together as a family about these fears would be invaluable and enriching. Processing through these different types of fears together as a family in case any of them would happen could help us overcome them.

The ten fears Stephen lists are:

Failure: I have not met a person yet who wants to fail in caring for someone. This fear of failure or not meeting the need can hinder us from trying at all.

Rejection: There are few things that hurt more than rejection, and if our care is turned down or dismissed, it can cut deep.

Lack: We care out of our reserves, and the fear of not having enough to care is a true concern. The fear of not having enough resources whether they are emotional, physical, spiritual, or financial can stop us in our tracks. The fear of lack is one of overvaluing what we do not have and undervaluing what we do have.

Criticism: Being criticized for the care you provide or being criticized for caring can be painful. Most of us try to avoid pain, so overcoming the fear of being criticized can be challenging.

Communicating: How we share that we care can be an obstacle to caring. It can be an obstacle that can stop us dead in our tracks.

Decision-Making: Making the decision about who to care for and how to care for them can also be a significant fear. No one starts off their day looking to make mistakes. The fear of making the mistake of choosing the wrong person or the wrong time can paralyze us into not doing anything.

Inadequacy: While lack is about not having enough resources, inadequacy is about not being enough. This fear is one of thinking that our natural talents, acquired abilities, and spiritual giftings are not enough given the situation and that God will not show up.

Risk-Taking: Caring for someone is a risk, no doubt about it. If you are fear-averse or want a sure thing, caring can provoke even more fear.

Standing Up: When you stand up and care for someone when it is not popular or in vogue, you are fighting against the fear of standing up. The fears that accompany it provoke concerns about how caring will impact me, my family, friends, community, and employment. The fear of standing up is real, and I would venture to say that at one time or another we have all given into this fear and regretted it.

Significance: We all want to belong, matter, and be known. We also want our caring to matter and be acknowledged. The fear of caring but not making a difference or caring and not seeing a change can hinder us from acting at all.

The Rest of the Story

You may be wondering how our family responded to the Carnaval celebration and the burning of the papier mâché man on a cross. My wife, Heather, had a great group of Christian friends who were equally disturbed by the events of the day. But none of these ladies were French. So how do you have a cultural conversation like this one without offending everyone involved? How do you remain courageous and not keep silent?

The ladies prayed about what they wanted to share and their motive behind wanting to share their perspective. Their desire was not to change the school, but rather to care for their children and offer a different point of view or perspective on the events of the day. They made an appointment with the principal of the school, and he agreed to meet with them.

Thankfully, the principal was very receptive to their concerns. He understood that Monsieur Carnaval looked like he was on a cross. And the kids throwing their sins written on a piece of paper at him was equally disturbing. He also remarked that most of the time, Monsieur Carnaval is not burnt but stored away for the next year's celebration. He also understood that it could be disturbing given the nature of the events of the day and the fact that recently there had been men burnt to death in similar fashion on the northern beaches of Madagascar.

The ladies ended the meeting by sharing that they were not going to try to stop the school from having the celebration. However, our families would not be able to participate the next year if the celebration would unfold in similar fashion. My wife and her friends were courageous on that day, and I will never forget it.

A Caring Family

Courage is the virtue that provides strength. Caring for others requires great courage. Without courage, we can often surrender to fear that moves us toward self rather than others. Stephen Blandino lists common fears as fear of failure, rejection, lack, criticism, communication, decision-making, inadequacy, risk-taking, standing up, and significance. Courage is not the absence of these fears but pushing through them to care for others.

The family provides a safe place for family members to experience caring for others with the support and strength provided by other family members. The importance of a home that values and helps build a foundation of courage is paramount. I would encourage you to consider these questions yourself and then finding a time to discuss them in an age-appropriate way with your family.

Natural Courage

1. Do you consider yourself a naturally courageous person?
2. How do you identify courage in yourself and family members and how can you help encourage them to grow in it?
3. What are some caring activities you can do as a family to build a foundation of courage from which to care for others?

The Tension

1. Does it take courage for you to care for others? If so, what are some of your fears?
2. Is controlling outcomes one of the blocks that keeps you from caring for others?
3. Who is someone you know who has the confidence and courage to care? What could you learn from them?

Foresight

1. Do you agree that the best predictor of the future is the past? What are some reasons you feel the way you do?

2. How can you support family members in their efforts to care for others and help them maybe avoid some pitfalls?

Realities

1. What are some ways you can help your family members see the realities of caring without them becoming jaded or disillusioned?

2. Do you have some stories that you could share about the realities of caring that could both be encouraging and insightful?

Overcomers

1. From Stephen's list of fears, were there a few that stood out to you?

2. Are there any of the fears that you have experienced caring for others?

3. What are some ways you could use this list of fears for conversation points with your family? What would those conversations sound and look like?

4 | RESILIENCY
The Virtue That Provides a New Normal

Our family has had the opportunity several times to travel to South Africa. Whether our travels were for organizational meetings, medical checkups, or getting Josiah's tonsils removed because the doctors in Madagascar were good at putting kids to sleep but not so good at waking them up after, we made it a point to get Mugg & Bean muffins. The muffins were one of the things we looked forward to getting each time we went and something we have built memories around.

In our minds, these muffins were not your typical muffins, or at least we did not think so. We believed these muffins were two or three times the size of a normal muffin and for some reason just tasted extraordinary. Mugg & Bean sold many different types of muffins, but our favorites were the triple chocolate chip and the strawberry walnut ones. And we would often eat several muffins while we were in South Africa and then take some home with us to Madagascar, freeze them, and eat them as a special treat.

Our normal pattern of buying the muffins to take back with us was to wait until we arrived at the airport for our departing flight. We thought it worked better to buy them there after we had checked in our luggage and had a free hand or two to carry them in. An added benefit was that the muffins were fresher, and we did not have to carry them and risk crushing the precious cargo on the way to the airport.

We had a system and it worked. And I know better than to change a system that works, but the last time we had flown out I had noticed that there was a Mugg & Bean on the other side of security and passport control. I thought we could buy the muffins there and it would be even better. One less thing to put on the scanner in security and one less conversation with the security agent about why I had so many muffins. So, on one occasion, I decided we would try my idea and wait and buy the muffins after passport control and security. You guessed it. It turned out to be a BIG mistake.

When we arrived at the airport, we checked in and dropped our checked bags off. On our way to passport control we walked past lots and lots of beautiful big fresh triple chocolate chip and strawberry walnut muffins and their glorious aroma. It was the land of milk and honey that we could see but not yet taste. These muffins looked delicious, and Heather asked if we should just go ahead and buy them, but I wanted to wait. My wife is a smart lady, and I should have listened. But I figured if they had them on this side of passport control, they would have them on the other side.

I was wrong. Way wrong. After going through passport control, we went straight to Mugg & Bean. I quickly realized the mistake I had made in waiting to buy the muffins. Gone were all the beautiful triple chocolate chip and strawberry walnut ones that we were waiting for. The only type of muffins they had left were carrot and lemon poppy seed. You may love carrot and poppy seed muffins, but my kids were truly disappointed. Needless to say, I was frustrated. I had made the wrong decision. I should have not changed our system. I now needed to find a way to fix it.

No dad wants to be the one who did not get the muffins for his kids, so I began to think of a way to get back through passport control to the land of milk and honey and the muffins that were on the other side. I thought I could go back out through passport control, buy the muffins, and then come back in through passport control for a second time. It sounded easy, achievable, and doable in the time I had before our flight departed. I asked a security guard if my plan was possible, and he affirmed that it was. He opened a security door for me so that I could go down a set of stairs to arrivals and go through visa and immigration with those getting off other planes.

The visa and immigration process went smoothly as there is no paperwork for a tourist visa for Americans when they arrive in South Africa. So, it was a few questions and a quick stamp and I was on my way. I went back up through the airport, found the triple chocolate chip and strawberry walnut muffins, bought a bunch of them, and then returned to the line at passport control. I was so proud of myself. I created a problem by not buying the muffins beforehand but had come up with a solution to solve the problem. I was feeling good.

When it was my turn for the preliminary passport and boarding pass check, my success turned to chaos. I reached into my pocket to get my passport and boarding pass only to realize I had all the passports and boarding passes. Not the wisest decision to take them all with me on the excursion, but I thought it would be okay. And it was okay until the lady at passport control told me I could only go through passport control once in twenty-four hours. At first, I thought she was joking. Unfortunately, she was not joking.

I tried to not let my face turn red and explained that my family was on the other side of passport control and that our plane was going to leave in about an hour. She said firmly that my family might be getting on that plane, but I would not. I shared that if this was going to be the case, I would need to get them their passports and boarding passes.

I then asked if she would consider giving their passports and boarding passes to them. She said there was no way she could take responsibility for the documents. I pointed to my family who we could both see on the other side of passport control and asked if I could then hand the documents to them. Her response was that I could give the documents to them myself in twenty-four hours when I went through passport control again the next day.

Resiliency

While on a walk many years after said muffin airport incident, to coincidently get some more Mugg & Bean muffins to take back to my son, my friend Butch, who is in the process of writing and doing research for a book he is writing, brought up the subject of resiliency.[23] Butch is a fellow West Virginian and has been a friend and mentor for many years, so when he asks a question, I intently listen. His question that day about resiliency made me realize that resiliency was not a virtue I ever considered or had given thought to until my mid-thirties.

I had spent the earlier years of my life avoiding negative hardships and stressors. And in all honesty, I have never particularly sought out experiences that are stressful, looked for circumstances that throw me off balance, or walked toward situations that I did not think would turn out in a positive way or how I thought they would. By not facing certain hardships and stressors head-on and intentionally processing them, I had limited the lessons I could learn from them and the resiliency I could have been building.

If I was continually avoiding stressors and hardships and not developing my resiliency muscle, I was surely not demonstrating and emulating resiliency to my family. What I now realize is that I was directly and indirectly communicating to them to avoid hard things. Ultimately, I had failed to recognize the value of stressors and hardships in my own life, and my weakness was not only impacting me and my resiliency but was also impacting those I love the most.

As Butch and I walked and talked that day, another thing that came to mind was that I often use resiliency as a broad term and fail to recognize that I could be resilient in one area of my life and be woefully weak in another area. There are also days that I feel resilient and on other days get frustrated and discouraged with the most trivial of circumstances.

Even though I began to consider and focus on resiliency in my thirties, I had failed to have conversations with my kids about what I have learned and the importance of resiliency, conversations about how I have learned to think of my resiliency as a tank. The way my tank is filled is through lessons learned from difficult situations, positive outcomes, a good night's sleep, healthy diet, regular exercise, having difficult conversations and coming out healthier on the other side, and relational and spiritual health. These are the ways I have found to grow in resiliency, and if I want my family to care for others, resiliency is a must.

Changing Understanding

Since my mid-thirties, when I started considering, studying, and building resiliency, I have definitely seen a shift in my understanding of what resiliency truly is. I used to put resiliency in the same category as being stubborn or hardheaded, something for which we, West Virginians, are known. Now being both stubborn and hardheaded does have some positive angles to it, but stubborn and hardheaded are weak descriptors of resiliency. And my inaccurate definition has led to some repetitive failures that I labeled as being resilient, but in reality were just unwise decisions and reactions that led to unwise stewardship of my time and resources.

Davis and Davis provide a healthier definition of resiliency when they share that it is the ability to bounce back to a "new normal" or area of health after facing a negative stressful event.[20] In their definition, resiliency involves change. It is not doing the same thing repeatedly expecting different outcomes. The change in my mindset about resiliency occurred when I started focusing on how I was different after a stressful, negative event or hardship and what I learned from it. This allowed me to have evaluative experiences rather than static repetitive ones.

Davis and Davis also share that adaptability is using our exposure to negative events to help us build up a hardiness to future negative events.[20] This once again highlights the possibility of positive change that can occur in us as we experience these negative events, but the positive change that can occur with adaptability is a possibility, not an assurance. It is a choice and involves intentionality and focus from us.

One way I have found to grow my resiliency and develop myself in a possible negative or difficult situation is through international travel. It may just be me, as I do seem to end up with the disgruntled security worker who wants me to put my thirteen-month-old son in the scanning machine by himself or the cheeky stewardess who tells me there is only one meal available, and I can take it or leave it, in just those words. Heather is convinced it is my magnetic personality.

Without a doubt, traveling internationally gives you the opportunity to see different places, eat amazing food, and experience life and cultures outside of your home country. But in my experience, there are all kinds of stressors and situations that can test your flexibility and adaptability, from language barriers, to delayed flights, to the guy in front of you who reclines in his chair for most of the ten-hour flight, to going through customs, to getting your suitcase in baggage claim and realizing it was put in a large blender on its way to your destination. There are just many ways that international travel can grow your resiliency.

After experiencing all of these things, I wanted to prepare my parents for their first trip to Madagascar, some of the unknowns and possible bumps in the road. I spent several weeks leading up to their departure sharing what had been pounded into my head, that being adaptable and flexible is a must for traveling and living overseas.

At that point in my life, my solution for dealing with the stressors and negative events was to travel with zero expectations. I had concluded that the less expectations I had, the easier travel and life was. So, I shared this with my dad, that the less expectations that he had about coming to Madagascar, the better. Just come and go with the flow. My dad responded that he was coming a long way around the world to have no expectations and just go with the flow. He was right, but how do we develop resiliency in our families to care and at the same time not become extremely frustrated and discouraged in the process?

Predictable Obstacles to Resiliency

Recognizing that I was going to need to continue to grow in resiliency during the pandemic, I began to devote more time and bandwidth to reading and listening to books about resilience. One of the books that really spoke to me was Jon Gordon's book, *The Garden*.[24]

In *The Garden*, Jon shares a spiritual fable about overcoming obstacles like fear, stress, and anxiety.[24] And in the process of overcoming these obstacles, Jon shares that we can develop increased levels of spiritual awareness and resilience.

I was recently able to interview Jon for the podcast to discuss *The Garden* in more depth and to ask him some questions that had been rattling in my heart and mind concerning resiliency.[25] Jon did not disappoint and once again I learned much from him.

Jon is a master communicator and I appreciated how he applied the lessons from the book to his personal life. Jon shared that there is a common pattern that the enemy of our souls uses to chip away at our resiliency and how if we allow this to go unchecked over time, we end up in mental and emotional places and states that we would have never imagined, wanted, or desired to be in.[25]

With the focus of this book being families modeling and emulating caring in their homes and communities so that they can then change the world one life at a time, I think it is valuable to consider some of the Ds (Doubt and Discourage) Jon shares about in the book that can chip away at our resiliency.[24] As I have thought and prayed about what Jon shared, I have added a few other Ds (Disorientation and Dissonance) that I have also found can limit my personal resiliency.

By examining these Ds, we can recognize a common pattern that the enemy of our souls uses and how these Ds impact our resiliency in a caring family. I have also included what I refer to as the antidote to these Ds or the power that Jesus gives us to overcome them and build resiliency.

Disorientation

Disorientation is the first D that I have personally experienced impact my resiliency and have witnessed impact other people's resiliency. I am not talking about disorientation like dementia, deliriums, or being drunk or high. But I am talking about the disorientation that occurs from stress and unmet expectations and assumptions when we are confused about how we got into a caring situation, what we are doing to care, is it appreciated and impactful, and our "why" for doing what we are doing.

For sure, there is no shame or guilt in being disoriented, and I believe that if you care frequently enough, you will eventually end up experiencing being disoriented. In my experience, families that can have conversations about being disoriented when caring are able to more readily recognize it and help each other develop resilience toward it.

Caring for someone often involves stress, emotions, good intentions, and a host of other feelings. None of these are bad things. However, an unexamined cocktail of these can throw us off balance, and that is when we can become disoriented and lose our perspective. If we are not vigilant and have not built up some level of resiliency toward disorientation, what was a momentary disorientation in caring can evolve into giving up or giving in. And I have seen some people who tried caring for others only to become disoriented and not like the feelings of instability it can create and quit caring altogether.

If you have ever been blindfolded and then spun around, you have some sense of what it feels like to be disoriented. As I was a kid when we would play these games, my stomach would feel queasy, and I would get a headache. The first thing I would do once the blindfold was removed was to grab ahold of something or somebody so I could fix my eyes on something unmovable and constant so I could reorient. And I believe this is one of the great-est benefits of caring as a family. When someone becomes disori-ented when caring, the family is there to grasp the family member so that they can focus on something constant.

That constant for me is my relationship with Jesus. He does not change, remains the same, and helps me regain my perspec-tive and orientation. He is my antidote against disorientation. My family has demonstrated to me that when I become disoriented, if I can pause and reorient on Him, I regain my balance and perspec-tive and am able to continue on in caring for others.

Doubt

The second D that can impact resiliency is doubt. Of all the enemies of our hearts, minds, and souls, doubt must be one of the most destructive and insidious. At least it has been for me. And when I begin caring for someone else and slowly begin to doubt the person I am caring for, doubt myself, or doubt the one I get strength from to care for others, a beautiful, rich opportunity can quickly become a destructive one.

My personal struggle with doubt often begins with question-ing my motives. When I am doubting my motives for caring, I begin to explore what my motivations were to start caring, what they are at the present time, the distance between the two, and how I arrived at this place. I often find figuring out my own moti-vations for caring to be a challenging task, but it is worth it and helps me develop resiliency in the face of doubt. If I can settle my motives, it helps me proceed with a clean heart and mind.

At times, I have also found myself doubting the motives of the person I am caring for. It is not something of which I am proud. And in my experience, I have not found trying to deduce the motives of someone else to be a productive process or healthy use of my time. With the knowledge that assigning motives to someone else's actions to be dangerous and unkind, I try to stop myself from going down this path any further, and it takes resiliency to stop myself.

The last thing I have found that I commonly begin to doubt when caring for someone is my capability or ability to care when the situation seems complex or complicated. Ultimately, this comes down to my doubt and lack of trust in God to provide me with the ability to care for them. I begin to doubt my natural talents, acquired abilities, and spiritual giftings, all things He has given to me to care for others.

My antidote to use against doubt is confidence or trust. The psalmist writes, "He will guide and direct me in the way I should go, and he will counsel me with his loving eyes upon me" (Psalm 32:8).[26] By placing my confidence in trust in the one that will guide, direct, and counsel me, I am able to build resiliency and stop myself before I go down the slippery, destructive path of doubt.

Dissonance

The third D that can impact resiliency in caring is dissonance. Dissonance occurs when I have two conflicting beliefs, such as I value people and want to care for them but because of doubt and disorientation I walk away from opportunities to care. I have experienced dissonance when I believed one thing but my actions demonstrated that I do not value what I say that I do.

And once dissonance sets in and gets a foothold, the mental and emotional battle ramps up as I often drift toward confabulations or lies that I honestly tell myself or conspiracy theories which are emotionally satisfying versions of reality that are based on lots of conjecture and me filling in the blanks with my imagination. I like to think of myself as a kind, considerate, and intelligent person, but it is amazing the things I have believed because of my inability to combat dissonance in my heart and mind.

The antidote that helps me build resiliency toward dissonance is truth-telling and having people in my life that will tell me the truth about what I am thinking. I know you are probably thinking that truth-telling is obvious and not a new or revolutionary idea. But if I am disoriented and doubting, truth-telling can become less obvious and less apparent. Having family discussions on the importance of truth-telling to combat dissonance is vital. Caring families can help combat lies told honestly and an imagination running wild.

Families can use T.H.I.N.K to guide conversations on truth-telling. I had never heard about T.H.I.N.K until my wife shared it with me. The T.H.I.N.K acronym was first developed to give guidance concerning civility when communicating on social media. It outlines that we can ask ourselves if what we are communicating is True, Helpful, Inspiring, Necessary, and Kind.[27] Although it was developed for what we share outwardly, it has been a valuable tool for me to consider what I am telling myself and to combat dissonance.

Discouragement

The fourth D, which I have found can erode my resiliency in caring is discouragement. If I am disoriented, doubting, falling into dissonance, and not using my antidotes to stop these three in their tracks, the next stop on the D train for me is discouragement. I begin to believe and internalize that I will never regain my orientation and my world will continue to spin out of control, that I cannot trust myself or others, and believe that the lies, conspiracy theories, and confabulations are reality.

Jon Gordon shares that the enemy of our souls knows that with Christ the enemy cannot beat us, so the enemy tries to get us to beat ourselves.[24] And I have experienced this myself and seen it happen to countless others. Jon shares an analogy from sports that resonates with me. When I played sports, I could not physically take opposing players off the court, but if they mentally took themselves out of the game and were on the sidelines, it was so much easier to dominate and win. And that is exactly what the enemy of our souls does to us in life which is much more important than a game. He uses discouragement to remove us from caring for others and fulfilling the mandate of loving and caring for our neighbor as we do ourselves.

I was searching for an antidote to use against discouragement and Jon Gordon provided it. Jon shares that we can battle discouragement by talking to ourselves rather than listening to ourselves. That is a powerful statement, speaking truth rather than listening to lies. And the greatest source of truth is scripture. Scriptures like Romans 15:13, "May the God of hope fill you with all joy and peace in believing, so that by the power of the Holy Spirit you may abound in hope," and Joshua 1:9, "Have I not commanded you? Be strong and courageous. Do not be afraid, and do not be discouraged, for the Lord your God will be with you wherever you go," have helped me build resiliency toward discouragement.[26] If parents can emulate and model speaking to themselves rather than listening to themselves, they can help their family grow in resiliency in caring and combat discouragement.

A Caring Family

Resiliency is the virtue that provides a new normal. Being able to bounce back from difficult life events and stressful experiences to a new normal is a skill and a blessing that can be demonstrated and modeled in the home. Resiliency is paramount for caring families, and parents can provide intentional opportunities in caring to help their children grow this resiliency muscle.

When faced with predictable roadblocks and obstacles like disorientation, doubt, discouragement, and dissonance, parents can model the positive antidotes that can be used against these. If children are given the opportunity to develop these antidotes early on, it will help them move through these common obstacles, continue to care, and arrive at a new normal. The importance of a home that creates an environment for family members to develop resiliency is vital for a caring life. I would encourage you to consider these questions concerning resiliency yourself and then discuss them in an age-appropriate way with your family.

Resiliency

1. How does avoiding negative or difficult situations limit our resiliency?
2. If a parent chooses to continually avoid difficult situations could this impact the rest of the family and their desire and ability to care?
3. What are some ways you could talk to your children and family members about resiliency and then begin to model it?

Changing Understanding

1. In what ways does resiliency differ from being hardheaded or stubborn?
2. How do you define resiliency?
3. Is there a family member that is resilient and what is the story behind their resiliency?

Disorientation

1. How does disorientation impact resiliency? Have you ever experienced disorientation when you were caring for someone?
2. What are some actions you can take to help provide stability for family members if they become disoriented while caring?
3. Where do you find your stability in the midst of disorientation?

Doubt

1. How is doubt destructive to a caring family?
2. Have you ever doubted your motives for caring or doubted the motives of the person you were caring for? How did you resolve this in your heart and mind?
3. Does Psalm 32 help increase your trust in God during times of doubt?

Dissonance

1. Have you ever experienced having two conflicting beliefs when it comes to caring?
2. How does truth-telling help you navigate these two conflicting beliefs?
3. Would you consider using the T.H.I.N.K acronym to help you battle against dissonance?

Discouragement

1. Have you ever experienced discouragement as a spiritual attack? What did you learn and how did it draw you closer to Jesus?

2. What are some ways you can help your children and family members when they become discouraged while caring for others?

3. How can you help your family learn to talk to themselves using scripture rather than listening to themselves?

4. What scriptures would be valuable to memorize as family to fight against discouragement?

5 | SPIRITUALLY FOCUSED
The Virtue That Provides
Hope and Creativity

Growing up, my family was at church when the doors opened, no questions asked. No debating. The Santmyires were there. For most of my childhood, we rode to and from church in a red, two-door 1972 Chevrolet (Chevy) Impala with a white vinyl top. When we would complain about sticking to the vinyl seats or the lack of air conditioning in the car, my parents were quick to remind us that the Chevy was an answer to their prayers.

Early on in their marriage and in the beginning days of starting a family, my parents needed an affordable, safe, and dependable car. They did not have much money and could not afford to go into debt for one. So, they prayed that God would provide the right car at the right price at the right time. And through a series of circumstances, God answered their prayers with the Chevy. That car was part of our family for twenty-plus years and the car that my sister and I learned to drive in.

I know I am dating myself, but I remember the time when wearing seat belts in cars was optional. The Chevy had basic seatbelts in it, but they were not nearly as comfortable as the ones today. And when you were riding in a car as big as the Chevy you felt like you had all the protection you needed in the size of the car, and if there was a quick stop or swerve in the road, my mom's right arm acted as the safety bar that kept us from hitting the dash or the front window.

Imagine a Friday evening and you are in this 1972 red Chevy Impala on a windy three-mile stretch of a West Virginia road that you knew like the back of your hand. Although there is a song about country roads taking you home, your experience is that those country roads are some of the windiest and are not the safest roads. The road you are on is no different, as it has a foot or two shoulder, which are often littered with fallen large rocks on the mountainside of the road and on the other side of the road there was no shoulder at all, just a guardrail that has to be continually repaired because the ground under it keeps giving way and tumbling down the mountain. You pray that if you ever need the guardrail, it will somehow keep you from going over the edge of the sharp decline into the trees below. But you pray you will never need to test it.

On this dark summer's evening you are going to church with your two young children. Your spouse had to work overtime and could not go, but you have responsibilities at church and must be there. With his absence in the car, your kids are happy to be able to sit in the front seat where they can see all the action.

Driving down the road past a curve, your headlights bring to your attention a single car about 200 yards away coming in your direction. The road is narrow and full of curves, but as you gaze ahead it appears the car is on your side of the road, the guardrail side. It does seem odd that it would be in your lane coming your direction. But you know this road has many twists and turns and the car is still a distance from you. Out of caution you begin to slow down some in case they are in the wrong lane thinking this would give them time to get into their lane of the road, the lane closest to the mountain.

As you continue driving, you are becoming more and more concerned as you now realize the car is about 100 yards from you and is no longer in your lane but is straddling the center yellow lines. You hear music blaring and notice there is a young man hanging out of the window screaming something but you are not able to understand. Your mind begins to race a little because you know there are several places that serve alcohol in the small town you are heading toward. Is it possible this could be a drunk driver?

You quickly look to your right and all you see is the silver shiny guardrail, and as you rapidly glance to your left there is nowhere to go there either. If you turn left, you will end up running into the mountainside, and turning to the right would mean running into the guardrail and possibly going over the side of the mountain. Recognizing the seriousness of this situation, you are increasingly concerned for your four-year-old daughter and one-year-old son who are beside you in the front seat.

As you have done in the past, you stretch your right arm out to hold them in place and use the left arm to steer the car. Your mind is now racing, and you look again praying that the driver has seen you and has changed course. If they have seen you, they have not moved from being in the middle of the road and are now coming straight at you at seemingly ever-increasing speed.

The car is not slowing down and is now less than twenty-five yards from you and you have nowhere to maneuver the car to get off the road and out of its way. They are truly taking their half of the road from the middle of it. The only thing you know to do is to continue to pray. You are lost for words but the word that you have not forgotten is the name of Jesus, and you begin saying the name of Jesus out loud and asking for Him to help. And then you hear the Holy Spirit speak to you, "Stop this car," and that is what you do. You stop the car in the road.

As you are praying, you look up once again and see the car is now ten yards from you, coming straight at you, and now blinding you with their headlights. The music blaring from the car is getting louder and louder. You pray louder and you hold your children back tighter in the seat. Glancing up, the car is now five yards from the front of your car, still coming straight at you, and all you can now see is its bright headlights. You continue to pray, put your head down on the steering wheel, tense up, and brace for the deafening shearing of metal and the impending impact.

You Cannot Give What You Do Not Have

One of the greatest challenges I see for families focusing on being or becoming a caring family is that a family cannot give what they do not have. How does a family find the strength and courage to care for someone else when they are tired and worn out because their schedule and pace of life has no margin in it? What does a family do when the person they want to care for does not look like them, sound like them, or act like them? How can you share love and compassion when your love and compassion tank is empty?

These are all really valid and poignant questions that may highlight some of the reasons families are making caring for others less and less common and prioritized. Families today are frequently exhausted and have little left in their love and compassion tanks to care for themselves, let alone for others. With the recognition of the fatigue, families have turned to TikTok for the hidden secrets of an efficient and effective life, only to fill the time and space they gained with more busyness.

Another joy and challenge for a caring family is the reality that the cultural landscape is becoming more diverse each and every day. With diversity comes many blessings, and at the same time caring for someone from a different cultural background in an intentional way can take more energy and more time. If families are already worn down, they can move away from choosing to invest the extra time and energy to care for someone who does not look and sound like them.

Ultimately, when you are exhausted and worn out it is harder and harder to have energy for others within the family, let alone outside the family. I 100 percent agree that caring for others takes time, energy, resources, and mental and emotional energy. Unless the family is being refreshed, recharged, and refilled, eventually their tank runs out, and when the tank is dry there is no energy left to use to care for themselves or others.

Refreshing through Remembrance

One of the lessons my parents taught me and a lesson I regret not focusing on more when Heather and I were raising our kids is how remembering with a heart of gratitude provides some of the most energizing and refreshing nourishment to a worn-down and weary soul. Heather would frequently ask me at dinner or when we were in the car together to tell a family story. But I often did not because I had spent my time and energy elsewhere during the day.

I missed opportunities to refresh my soul and my family's and the opportunity to remember that the one who has done miracles in our family's past is also the one doing miracles today. And the one who does miracles has also promised to restore our souls. He is ready and willing to refill us if we are willing to slow down enough to rest and feed from his goodness.

One story that my father shared that reminded us of God's goodness and love for us was when he was burnt as an 8-year-old child. My grandparents had told my dad to not play with fire and matches, but he had just got a new cowboy outfit and was so excited to show it off to his friends. What is a cowboy without a good horse and a good campfire? A horse was not within reach, but a campfire was.

My dad and his friend found some wood to make a fire with but were having trouble getting the fire started. So, they decided to add some gasoline to the wood. If you know anything about gasoline, you know that when you handle it, oftentimes you end up with the fumes on your hands and clothes. It was no different for my dad. The fire lit well with the gasoline, but when he got close to it, his clothes caught on fire.

As the clothes burned, they melted to the skin on his legs. Eventually, he was able to get the fire out, but the damage had already been done. His parents took him to the hospital where the doctors had no choice but to remove the clothes, but as they removed his clothes they also removed multiple layers of the skin on his leg, exposing the muscles and tendons.

My dad shared that he was in great pain and agony. Infection eventually set in and the doctors shared with my dad and his parents that the safest course of action would be to try skin grafts but they were not sure that the grafts would take. If the grafts did not take, they would need to amputate his leg below the knee.

As you can imagine, this was devastating news to both my dad and my grandparents. After trying the skin grafts and the grafts not taking, the doctors spoke with my grandparents. They were going to have to decide on whether to keep his leg or amputate it, and the next twenty-four hours or so would be critical. My grandparents asked the doctor if they could wait twenty-four hours before making any decisions. They were going to ask their friends at church to fast and pray that God would do a miracle and take the infection away and heal my dad's leg.

The doctors rebandaged my dad's leg and told my grandparents that they would give it twenty-four hours more before making any more decisions. Over the next twenty-four hours, many fasted and prayed. When my grandparents returned to the hospital the next day, the doctors removed the dressing and to their startled disbelief, the infection was gone and in its place was a thin layer of healthy tissue. It was nothing less than a miracle, a miracle that my parents reminded me of and that I was reminded of every time I saw the large white patch on his leg from the skin graft.

My parents often slowed our family down and spent time telling stories like this one, of how there was a need in the family and God provided. Each time they did this, it was refreshing to our souls. It provided energy and strength to face the day, energy and strength to care for others as God had cared for us.

Everything Is Spiritual

I like to consider myself an aging athlete. My better athletic days are long in the rearview mirror as I fight the process of time. Even though I am slowing down, I do enjoy running in an occasional 5K race, and have run a marathon and a few half marathons. Some of my greatest family memories are from running in these types of races like running the Disney marathon with my sister Beth and friend Zach, to running local races with my wife Heather, to running races with both my wife and kids to raise money and awareness for missions. I know I am not going to win or set any land speed records, but I do enjoy being with other people and combining it with exercise. And the exercise part allows me to eat more apple pie. Apple pie = My love language!

Another thing I like about running in races is you frequently get a shirt for participating. It is a mark that you competed and were part of the event. The shirts are fun to wear and I have found them to be a great conversational piece. The race shirt that had first place for the most comments and best conversation starter was the Moonshine Classic. I got lots of raised eyebrows and questions about my West Virginia roots and how much of the moonshine I was drinking during the race.

The Moonshine Classic shirts were the most commented on one until I ran in a race a few years ago put on by a church that my friend and mentor pastors. The shirt from this race was atypical in that it did not have the name of the race on the front of it, but simply had *Everything is Spiritual* on it.

I have worn a lot of shirts in my forty-six years of life, but this shirt with *Everything is Spiritual* has gotten more remarks and comments than any shirt I have worn. People have stopped me in airports, in shopping malls, in restaurants, on the street and will often ask, "What does your shirt mean?" Another common question is, "Do you really believe that everything is spiritual?"

I honestly was wearing the shirt because I liked the color, but in the process of considering and pondering whether I really believed that *Everything is Spiritual*, which I do, I have become more and more convinced that one of the most spiritual things that we can do is care for someone else. Caring is a profoundly spiritual act and one of the foundations for the Christian life, and I wonder if that is another reason that families have moved away from caring because they are unsure or uncomfortable with the spiritual nature of it.

We see over and over again that Jesus modeled and demonstrated love and caring for others. As He did this, the person, the family, or the community did not just change physically, but individuals, families, and communities changed spiritually. As sickness and darkness were pushed aside, His acts changed the spiritual atmosphere. Jesus demonstrated that caring is paramountly spiritual.

As a parent, I could have done better connecting the dots for my kids on why our family valued caring for others. I could have done better making that connection that caring was not just a good act or act of kindness but was a spiritual act following the example that Jesus set for us. I left gaps that I think they understood, but I wish I would have explained why I was putting sutures in someone's head in our kitchen or why I was traveling to remote areas to provide care. The reason we valued caring in our family was that it was a spiritual act and my way of sharing the love of Christ in a practical, tangible way.

My encouragement for you as a parent and as a family is to put sutures in people in your kitchen. Just kidding! I do not recommend it. I do recommend that you not miss the opportunities to explore, explain, and discuss the reasons why you care and how caring is a spiritual act. Do not leave the reasons why you care for others up to chance or questioning, but clearly explain that caring is one of the most spiritual things you can do as you follow the example of Jesus.

Recognizing That Caring Is Spiritual Increases Creativity

I am a habit, rhythm, and discipline-type guy. Once I get into a habit or rhythm, I hate to break out of it. This quality has some positives and negatives to it. One positive is that I am able to get things done and focus. Another positive is once I am convinced it is hard to move me from my conviction. On the negative side is that the habit, rhythm, discipline, and conviction seem to suck any creativity out of my thinking. I can be stuck in a way of caring and not considering other creative options. Please hear me. I am not saying that creativity and discipline are mutually exclusive, but I have found them really hard to pair. I seem to be one a lot more than the other.

By acknowledging that caring is spiritual, families can open up the door to the opportunity for increased creativity. The God of the universe who created the world is infused into caring when we consciously and purposefully ask for His wisdom and direction. It is quite an amazing thing for families to ask the God who created the world to give them creative insight into how to care for someone and then listen to what God has to say.

Maybe you are uncomfortable with the idea of asking God to give you and your family creative insight. It is also possible that you as a parent do not feel capable of clearly hearing God for yourself, let alone to give your family guidance on how to care for someone else. Or maybe you have experienced someone sharing that they heard from God and you and everyone else knew they must have gotten their wires crossed when they thought they were hearing from God.

These are all understandable thoughts and feelings. As you invite the Creative God into the caring situation, I would encourage you to say a prayer as a family like this one.

Dear Jesus,

Your word says that the noble make noble plans and by noble deeds they stand. With a pure heart and open mind, our family desires to care for _____. We want to demonstrate that they are known, matter, and belong, and that we see the God-given dignity You have placed in them. So we ask you to give us creative wisdom and insight as we plan to care for them so that our plans will be noble and honoring to them and You. And when we do what you have asked us to do, help us to be confident that we are doing what you have asked us to do. Amen.

Once you have prayed a prayer similar to this, then spend time in the hours and days ahead listening and sharing what each person is sensing God say. I think you will be amazed as God gives creative ideas on how to care.

You may be thinking this asking and listening to God does not sound enjoyable but rather sounds painful. How do you know if you are hearing God's voice? What if you decide to do something and you heard God wrong? Will you permanently scar your kids if you mess this up? Doesn't God have more important things to do other than helping us figure out the details on how to care for others?

Pastor Ryan Ingram shares some powerful points about listening to God. I believe these points help each of us begin to hear what God is saying in a clearer way.[27]

1. God is nearer to you than you think and His nearness demonstrates that He wants to speak to you.

2. God is interested in the details of your everyday life, so ask Him about them.

3. God will not compete for your attention. Give Him time and space to speak.

4. Resist the fear of asking God to speak to you because you are afraid of what He will say or ask of you.

5. God can speak to you in an audible voice but most likely will speak to you through His Word, Christlike friends, dreams, the whisper and inner voice of the Holy Spirit, and through His creation.

6. If you have heard something that is for someone else's good, takes sacrifice and courage from you, and takes faith to act upon, it is most likely God speaking to you.

7. When you are doubtful that you are hearing God clearly, ask Him to confirm, with those you trust, what you are sensing that He is saying to you.

8. Be intentional about the language you use when sharing what you are hearing from God. Use language like "I sense God saying" or "I feel prompted" rather than "God told me." You cut off feedback from others when you state "God told me."

9. When you step out in faith, expect God to show up.

10. Do not just expect Him to show up but make space for God to show up.

And after you have prayed, listened, and shared, then go, do, and care. Keep in mind Philippians 4:8–10. "Finally, brothers and sisters, whatever is true, whatever is noble, whatever is right, whatever is pure, whatever is lovely, whatever is admirable—if anything is excellent or praiseworthy—think about such things. Whatever you have learned or received or heard from me or seen in me—put it into practice. And the God of peace will be with you."[26] It may not all go as you had planned, and you may not get it right every time, but rest in the promise that His peace will be with you.

The Rest of the Story

With your head on the steering wheel and your body tensed up, bracing for the impending impact, a sudden peace comes over you, a peace you cannot explain with words or emotions, peace that made you realize that there was someone in control of your life that was not you. A split second passes and there still is no impact. You quickly lift your head from the steering wheel, and miraculously the car is no longer in front of you, but you can still hear the music blaring. What had happened?

You hear a voice telling you to look behind the car and you turn to look. When you do, you see the tail end of your car touching the tail end of the car that had been coming straight at you and can see the young men in the car. You quickly turn back forwards and, trembling, make your way down the road to church thanking God for His miraculous power.

During my years at home, my mother would tell us this story at opportune times, times of wondering, times of doubting, times of uncertainty. And this story reminded me that Jesus performed a miracle on that road that evening. He saved our lives on that dark road, and I knew I could trust Him. My mother told this story because she never wanted our family to forget that God is with us and God is for us and for us to remember He is performing miracles in our lives each and every day.

In the past when I have shared this story with others, people who have never driven on that road have tried to give possible logical reasons for what happened, speculations and hypotheses. All I know is my mother, sister and I faced certain death that day, but He performed a miracle.

A Caring Family

Spiritually focused is the virtue that provides hope and creativity. We are spiritual beings with a past, present, and eternal future. And caring is a truly spiritual act. Parents have the space and time to help their children learn to hear God's voice and learn to follow what He is saying. Recognizing that God is nearer than we think, He wants to speak to us and is interested in our everyday lives and the lives of others, He will not compete for our attention so we need to provide space for Him to speak and for us to listen, and knowing He wants to show up in our lives should encourage us to be more interested in listening to Him. Healthy families provide fertile ground for children to hear God's voice and be guided in obeying it.

The importance of understanding the spiritual nature of our lives and how that impacts caring is essential for a caring family. I would encourage you to consider these questions yourself and then discuss them in an age-appropriate way with your family.

You Cannot Give What You Do Not Have

1. How does the statement "you cannot give what you do not have" sit with you?
2. What are some rhythms and practices you can have in your family life to model not being worn out and tired?
3. Is it easier or more difficult to care for someone who is different than you are? If it is more difficult, how can your family find the time and energy to bridge this gap?

Refreshing through Remembrance

1. How does remembering with a heart of gratitude provide nourishment to your soul?
2. What are some stories from your family's history where God provided?
3. Can you begin to share these stories more frequently as a source of encouragement to those in your family?

Everything Is Spiritual

1. Do you believe "everything is spiritual?" What are some reasons you feel the way you do?
2. How is caring for someone else a spiritual act?

3. What are some ways you can begin focusing your family on the spiritual nature of caring for others?

Recognizing That Caring Is Spiritual Increases Creativity

1. How does recognizing that caring is spiritual increase creativity?
2. Do you think your family currently is creative in how you care for each other and those outside your family?
3. Could you commit to begin to pray as a family about how you can creatively care for others?

Listening to God

1. What has been your experience when it comes to listening to God?
2. What are two or three of the points that Pastor Ryan Ingram shares that made you pause for a minute to reflect?
3. How can you make space to listen to God and space for Him to show up?

6 | PATIENCE
The Virtue That Provides Perspective

When I was a kid, spring was one of my favorite times of year. I enjoyed moving out of the dull and dreary days of winter and the entering of the warmer and longer days that brought me closer to the end of school and the warm days of summer. Spring also brought with it my dad and I's annual trout fishing trip to the Smoke Holes on the South Branch of the Potomac.

In the first few years of our fishing trips, we did just that. A lot of fishing but not as much catching as either he or I would have liked. We tried different lures and baits, fishing on different sides of the stream, fishing with waders and without waders, and fishing early morning and late into the evening. The results were similar, lots of drowned worms, tangled lines, and not very many fish to show for it. We would come home a little discouraged, but by the time the following year rolled around, we had forgotten the failures of the year before and were full of expectation.

One year when I was twelve, my dad and I had a well-thought-out plan that we had been strategizing on during the winter months, and we were ready and confident that we were going to catch more trout. The drive from our house in Wiley Ford to our favorite fishing spot, Smoke Holes along the South Branch of the Potomac, takes about two hours depending on who is driving, how strong the driver is feeling the trout calling out to them, and how much the passenger can endure the curves in the road without getting car sick. And my habit now that I can drive is to drive a little faster and when we arrive at the stream, I want to be the first one with my line in the water.

On this trip, my dad wanted to take me to a spot on the stream where he had caught fish in the past and had water flow at the speed we liked. We both like moving water but not fishing in rapids. When we arrived, I was on the stream in no time. I surveyed the water and cast my line into the spot that looked most promising. Within seconds, I had hooked into something big. I was in disbelief as this was my first cast, but I began to yell for my dad to come because I could not control my excitement. The fish fought hard, and I was determined to land it. If it was as large as it felt, it would be the largest fish I had ever caught and maybe even a trophy-sized trout.

After several minutes of reeling and fighting the fish, my dad and I got a good look at it. I could not believe my eyes; it was a big rainbow trout. The plan Dad and I had been thinking of all winter had worked. I was about to land the biggest fish I had ever seen, let alone had the opportunity to catch. Although it was not pretty, I eventually got it out of the water and onto dry land.

My dad and I were both beaming with excitement and pride. We did it! We caught a big rainbow trout. I quickly put the trout on a stringer and placed it back in the water. As I was watching it, dad shared that we might as well keep fishing because there might be another big fish in there where that one was.

We both went back to fishing and talking about the fish I had just caught. Within ten minutes, we heard a voice coming down the path to the stream saying hello and asking how we were doing. My dad's comment was that someone must have seen me catch the trout and now they were moving in to fish beside us. Unfortunately, that would have been the better case scenario than what unfolded.

As I turned to look at the person on the path who had greeted us, I saw that it was not another fisherman but a West Virginia Division of Natural Resources Officer (WV DNR). I am sure DNR officers are great people, but not who I am looking to talk to when fishing.

At first, he was nice enough and asked us again how we were doing and if we had caught any fish. I was excited and a little too proud to show him the rainbow trout that I had caught. He looked at the fish, slowly bent down, proceeded to take it off the stringer and helped it swim away. I was shocked and stunned. I asked him why he had just let my fish go. How could he do that?

The WV DNR officer responded that I had illegally caught the fish. He shared that we were fishing in a designated Catch and Release (C&R) area and that we were not allowed to keep fish until June. This was the first year for C&R on this part of the stream and my dad and I had no idea that we were fishing illegally.

We knew that the WV DNR had marked some of the stream as C&R and we had looked for the signs that marked the restricted areas but did not see any. We tried to explain this to the officer, but he did not seem to be convinced. He stated that we had driven past a sign that clearly marked where C&R started, and he could not see how we missed it unless we "intentionally" missed it.

The officer then asked what I had used to catch the fish and I pointed to the bait we were using. He proceeded to tell me that

I had caught the trout on illegal bait using a barbed hook. Both the bait and the barbed hooks were illegal on this section of the stream. As the game warden saw it, I had committed at least three crimes catching the fish. I was twelve years old and had never committed a crime before and now had committed three crimes in the matter of ten minutes.

My dad and I were both perplexed by the unfolding of the events. We were higher than we could be without drugs when I caught the fish, but now were lower than we could have imagined. The officer shared that I did not need to worry because he was not going to charge me with the crimes. But he was going to need to have a conversation with my dad in his patrol vehicle. The officer told me that I would need to wait by the stream and be . . . patient. I did not like being patient before then, but this cemented my dislike of the virtue.

Patience: The Love-Hate Relationship

Internally, patience is a virtue I think all of us would agree has value and merit. And Christians know it as one of the fruits of the spirit that define the life of a disciple of Christ. At the same time it is and has been one of the hardest virtues of a caring family for me to model in my own family and personal life. I love the benefits and fruit of patience but have continually struggled with the practice of patience. Author M. J. Ryan shares:

"Patience gives us self-control, the capacity to stop and be in the present moment. From that place we can make wise choices. Patience helps us be more loving toward others. more at ease with the circumstances of our lives, and more able to get what we want. It constantly rewards us with the fruits of maturity and wisdom: healthier relationships, higher quality work, and peace of mind. It accomplishes magic by bringing together three essential qualities

of mind and heart that allow us to be our best: persistence, serenity, and acceptance."[28]

Sign me up each and every day, morning, afternoon and night,
and twice on Tuesdays for the fruits of patience like more maturity and wisdom, healthier relationships, higher quality work,
and peace of mind. For sure, I want to be more loving and caring
toward others. Constant rewards, yes, I want constant rewards also.

Considering all patience offers and can produce in my life, the
question is why do I continually struggle with it and not model
patience well for my family as I care for them and as we have cared
for others? I love what patience accomplishes in and through me
but the day in day out, minute by minute act of patience is something I continue to battle. And demonstrating patience to my
family when it comes to caring for them and others is something I
desire to develop and to flow from me supernaturally.

I say supernaturally because naturally, impatience is what flows
from me toward others. The reality of "what is in us, comes out of
us" is probably never more evident than in my battle with impatience. Impatience must be in me because it frequently comes out
of me.

Those that know me best would admit that I can move at a
hurried pace, and most of the time I seem to move at a hurried
pace with a smile both on my heart and on my face. I want to
know more than I know today, and I wanted to know it yesterday.
I want to progress each and every day, measuring today's progress
against the past and what I hope to see in the future. And I could
continue with an ever-increasing list about my impatience, but
the real struggle is that I can often rationalize my impatience, letting my mind win over my heart.

I have found that given enough time I can rationalize most
things, but it does not make the things I rationalize right or bene-

ficial. I can build a case for why there is dissonance between what I know to be true about patience and what my actions are demonstrating that I believe about patience. I have rationalized my lack of love for patience by labeling it old-fashioned or outdated. A virtue that is not suited for the fast-paced and instant society we live in.

A quick scroll on the internet or glancing at the news lets us know just how impatient the world we live in is becoming. But I cannot blame the world for my lack of patience. I have to take responsibility for my own actions. Whether that is the impatience of sending an email and becoming irritated that I have not received a reply within an hour or sending a text message and seeing that the person I messaged has seen it and is typing. Just not typing to me. Or like I did the other day, when I pulled into the shorter lane at the gas station and performed acrobatics to stretch the gas hose to the other side of my car because I did not want to wait in the proper line that had the pump on the same side as my gas tank. Go ahead and judge. I know, it's pretty sad.

These examples of my lack of patience are not the end of the world, but they do signal a larger problem that is not only impacting emails, texts, and gas lines but is also impacting how I love and care for others. Caring requires time and patience. And families that are driven by action and do not have time or patience can find it trying to care for others.

Parenting Fail 1043

When we transitioned to Kenya, the impatient parent that I can be thought it would be great for my kids to jump into activities at their new school. Now, I had never switched schools at their age, let alone switched countries, but for some reason, I thought the quicker they jumped into all their school had to offer the better. I did have good intentions, but it was a failure on my part.

My son has been kicking a ball since he could walk and I thought joining the soccer team at his new school would help him meet friends, adapt, and assimilate. I could tell he was a little hesitant the first day to stay for practice, but I encouraged him to do it anyway. I was going against what he thought was best because of my lack of patience and my desire for them to quickly get adjusted. Right motive, wrong heart.

One parental lesson I had already learned, but chose to ignore again, was that pushing my kids to do something rarely, if ever, produced a positive result for them or for our relationship. In fact, I cannot think of a time I used parental authority to get them to do something, excluding chores or the like, that I did not regret after. Pushing them to do things often ended up with both of us being frustrated and irritated with each other, and some of my biggest regrets as a parent have been when my lack of patience won out and I pushed anyway.

Despite all of this and what I knew about pushing them to do things, my son agreed to stay for soccer practice. When he came home from the first day of practice, I could see the concern on his face, but I tried to gloss it over. I told him and myself it would get better. All things get better with time, right? Wrong, some things get worse over time.

Anyway, I was more focused on the letter of commitment that we would both need to sign if he was going to play on the soccer team and tried to shift the focus toward that. We discussed the letter of commitment which outlined athletes would follow the school rules, attend practice, and prioritize academics. And we both hesitantly signed it.

After the second day of practice, we both realized that I had pushed him into something that may have been best for my misguided idea for a quick transition but was not best for him. My parental impatience was forcing him into a situation that was not going to be healthy for him during this season of transition. After some more discussion, we both now agreed playing soccer was not what was the best for him.

Courageously and maturely, he went to the coach and tried to share that he would not be joining the team or staying for practice. The coach asked him to think about it and come back the next day. Respectfully, he did think about it and was still convinced this was not the right thing for him at this time. So he went back to the coach who was still not convinced that he should not play on the team. Kindly, the coach tried to come up with a plan so that my son would have time to adjust and also stay on the team.

Following two meetings with my son and the coach which resulted in a stalemate, I decided I needed to go into school, see the coach, and admit that this situation was my mistake, not my son's. My lack of patience led me to an uncaring decision, and I needed to own up to what I had done.

Although a pastor's sharing of the following is for a different context, I wish I would have had this at hand before my impatient soccer decision. Having memorable guidance on making decisions when it comes to family is vital. A pastor shares:

1. If it is not good for him, it is sin.
2. If it is not good for her, defer.
3. If it is not good for you, no can do.
4. If it is not good for them, it should be condemned.[29]

Considering these four statements helps me move from my impatient and selfish heart to one that considers and thinks of others regardless of whether it fits into my timeframe.

Waiting Is an Action Verb

I was recently walking through a crisis and found myself wanting to do something. I felt the pull of falling back on my dad's advice of "doing something even if it is wrong." I would like to tell you my motives were pure and right. But the real reason that I wanted to do something was that the inner anxiety of being patient, waiting, and trusting was eroding at my inner peace.

During those days and hours, I sensed God sharing with me that "waiting is an action verb." I did not get much more than that, but it has made me reconsider how I view waiting and how I could have modeled patience better in our family. I do not know why I never considered it to be an action verb, but somehow I had always perceived being patient and waiting as inactivity and lack of progress.

By definition, waiting is not taking an action until certain conditions are met. For instance, I wait at a stop light until the light turns green. I sit in the waiting room until it is my turn to go back into the examining room. I wait outside of my kids' school to pick them up. I sit and wait on a plane while traveling to get to my destination. And I wait in line at the security checkpoint trying to get to my boarding gate.

If you are ever flying with me, you will be waiting longer in the security line if you are behind me. I will make a very long story short, but on one trip I had forgotten my hard drive in my friend's car. I had some extra time and asked him to bring it back to me at the airport. I retrieved the hard drive from him and then proceeded to go through security again, only to be taken to an undisclosed room where I had to strip down to only my underwear as the border patrol officers looked for some object that "they knew I had." But I had no idea what they were looking for. I waited in the center of the room standing in my underwear as they tried to find "it." To this day, I still do not know what "it" was, but 1.5 hours later I left the undisclosed room feeling like I was on Candid Camera.

Ultimately, waiting is not taking a certain action, but it does not mean a state of total inactivity. While waiting at the stop light, I can be listening to music, talking to those in the car with me, talking to myself, praying, and sipping on a Chick-fil-A Cookies and Cream milkshake. These are all action verbs, things I can be doing. But somehow, in the times of waiting I concentrate on the things I cannot do rather than on the things I can do, and that is where the impatience seems to kick in for me.

One of the things I would encourage families to do is to teach their kids and model waiting as an action verb. It requires the persistence, serenity, and acceptance that M.J. Ryan writes about, and focusing on what we can do in times of waiting decreases impatience and can increase our trust.[29]

The Rest of the Story

I waited patiently by the stream to hear the verdict of what the officer was telling my dad. When my dad got out of the car, I realized it was not good. The officer had fined him for three infractions and told him he needed to go straight to the courthouse to see the judge. West Virginians take our trout seriously!

We made our way to the courthouse and met with the judge. He also told me that I needed to sit and be patient while he talked with my dad. I could hear through the door though as he said the fine would be $126 or equal to two days of my dad's salary. The judge was less than kind, making comments throughout about how railroaders had lots of money so this should not be a problem, and he made a comment about the red Chevy and how a car like that was not cheap. I think the worst was when he gave my dad the option of spending two nights in jail in lieu of paying the fine.

Although he could have, my dad never shared with the judge that I was the one who actually caught the fish. My dad modeled patience that day. He was patient with me while I caught the fish, with the officer as he talked with him in the patrol car, and with the sarcastic judge. We left the courthouse with a piece of expensive paper instead of my trophy trout, but the biggest thing I left the courthouse with was recognizing I had a patient and kind dad.

A Caring Family

Patience is the virtue that provides perspective. Some might consider patience to be an old-fashioned virtue, but it is highly valued and produces exceptional fruit in our lives. Patience offers fruits like maturity and wisdom, healthier relationships, higher quality work, and peace of mind. Although it produces the fruit many desire in their lives, developing this virtue in an instant society and fast-paced world can be challenging. If we desire to have a caring family, patience is a must. Families that are driven by action and do not set aside time to listen to others will need to slow down and learn that waiting is an action verb. And when families demonstrate having more time and space and intently listen to others, they will see that patience truly makes them more of a caring family.

The power of patience in our caring lives is often not discussed. But our relationship with patience impacts us one way or another. I would encourage you to consider these questions about patience yourself and then discussing them in an age-appropriate way with your family.

Patience

1. Do you have some stories from your family about patience?
2. Are these stories that your family looks back to in fondness, embarrassment, or somewhere in between?
3. Who is the most patient person in your family? What are some reasons you chose them?

Patience, the Love-Hate Relationship

1. With all the benefits of patience, why do we struggle with it?
2. How does patience impact caring?
3. What are discussion points your family could talk about when it comes to caring for yourselves and others?

Parenting Fail 1043

1. How do you model patience in your family?
2. Have you ever pushed your kids into doing something only to recognize patience would have been a better choice?
3. How does caring for your kids with patience impact how they will care for others?

Waiting Is an Action Verb

1. How can the inner anxiety of wanting to do something impact your actions to care?
2. Do you agree that waiting is not a state of total inaction?
3. In an instant society, what are some ways you could model waiting in your home?

7 | TRANSFORMATIONAL AWARENESS
The Virtue That Provides
Growth and Change

Imagine it is 1991 and you are getting ready to turn fifteen years of age. The days leading up to your fifteenth birthday are full of excitement and anticipation as you cannot wait to begin learning how to drive. You live in the great state of West Virginia where you can get your learner's permit at fifteen, license at sixteen, and do not even need to take driver's education. You can almost taste the opportunity to drive and the freedom that goes with it.

You mark your fifteenth birthday on the family calendar so your mom can plan to take you to the Division of Motor Vehicles (DMV) so you can take the written test which will allow you to get your learner's permit. You have studied the driver's handbook like millions of people before you and know that many of those same people have passed a similar test, but you are still nervous. The hand signals, what to do when a school bus stops in front of you, and all the other important points you have been told to study in preparation for the written test are all clear in your mind.

What you have not factored in is the first step in the process, the visual acuity test. You will need to take and pass it, or you will not get to proceed to the written test. For most people, the visual acuity test is just a formality. It is more than a formality for you and will be a big challenge because you know your eyes have not been good for quite some time.

Your near vision is just fine but seeing things at a distance has progressively proven to be more and more difficult. You can see objects but do not necessarily see the details of the objects. For instance, you know that trees have leaves but from a distance all you see is a large green object. You also know that a basketball rim has a net attached to it, but when you are shooting the basketball, you can only see the thin outline of orange for the rim. And you can see people from a distance but are in no way able to distinguish who they are unless you recognize their voice or mannerisms.

The pain of not being able to see has not grown more painful than the story you have told yourself about the embarrassment of being fifteen years old and having to wear glasses. And you believe there is no way you would ever be able to touch your eye and put a contact lens into it. Consequently, you have become creative in developing a work-around for most situations which require you to see things at a distance.

So in math class, you refuse to move forward where you could actually see the writing on the black board and continue to sit in the back of the classroom where all you can see is that the board is black. You know one of the guys in the back of the class struggles with math and quickly find out he has great vision. A deal is made with him where he will read the problems to you, you solve them, and then you give him the correct answers. It is a deal that plays on both your strengths.

Even though the school requires a yearly visual acuity test, you have quickly found a way to maneuver around it. Normally, everyone is lined up in alphabetical order according to their last name. One by one each person sits in a chair, looks into a projector-type instrument, and the nurse asks them to repeat what they see line by line. You have learned that all you have to do is memorize the letters, the order they are stated in, and the corresponding line they go on. Thankfully, the person in front of you is blessed with great eyes, and year after year, you repeat what he says and pass with flying colors. You are told you have 20/20 vision, but you know there is no way this is true.

But on this day at the DMV there will be no work-around for the vision test. A kind female officer who oversees the testing process asks you to fill out a form and return it to her. She will then give your number so you can proceed to the visual acuity test. That is when your heart does a little flutter. A vision test! You were not planning on a vision test. You know that barring some miracle, this is where your chance at getting a learner's permit will end.

But you are not too dismayed. The contraption for the vision test is the exact same one the school nurse uses at your high school. You remember the order of the letters and remember the process. All you will have to do is pretend to look into it and give the letters you already know. After filling out the form, you sheepishly walk up to the lady, give her your completed paper, and wait your turn.

There are about twenty people in the small waiting area and you now realize they will all have a front row seat to your vision test. The police officer asks you to approach the contraption and read the 3rd line. You look into it and recite D, S, F, and H.

You look up and recognize the officer now looks a little irritated. He asks you to go again and read to him what you see. The letters you remember are D, S, F, and H and you cannot see anything in the contraption. So, you repeat the letters again in that order.

As you glance up toward him, his body language lets you know he is becoming more frustrated with you by the minute. This is supposed to be the perfunctory part of the process, and you are taking too long. And he is growing impatient.

He shares his frustration with the female officer who has taken your completed form. You hear the shuffling of the people in the waiting room and turn to look, and they are looking back at you. Your mother tells you to be serious and do what they are asking you to do. The problem is, you are being serious.

The female officer asks to speak with you, pulls you to the side, and communicates that you need to stop goofing off. She is kind about it, but you know she is not in a joking mood. She shares that if you are not able to get it correct on the third try, you will not be able to take the written test. Her encouragement is to go back to the contraption and read what you see.

You have now realized that the contraption they use for their vision test must not have the letters in the same order as the one at school. You intently concentrate, squint as hard as you can, and try some different letters. This time you voice O, C, B, and I. And you are quickly met with a voice loudly pronouncing to everyone in the room, "He failed." To say you are embarrassed is an understatement.

The female officer calls you back over and asks for your mother to come up with you so she can have a chat. You are even more embarrassed when she shares that there are no letters on the vision test, only numbers! You have repeatedly given all letters. Who had ever heard of a vision test with only numbers? Evidently, they had. You leave the DMV without a learner's permit and with the encouragement to make an appointment for an eye exam so you can get some glasses so you will be able to read the numbers on your return visit to the DMV.

Transformational Awareness

If awareness was just as easy as getting a set of glasses that could correct how we perceive ourselves, how we perceive others, how we recognize the dynamics between ourselves and others, and how we see where God is in the spaces between us, awareness would be a lot easier. But unfortunately, there are no glasses we can purchase to help us with the awareness I am writing about, which is an essential virtue for a caring family.

And although I believe that awareness is of great value and a virtue necessary for developing a caring family, I must admit that not everyone does think it is vital. And I add "transformational" to the word awareness and the virtue becomes more challenging to grow, develop, and model personally and within the family.

I write about the challenging nature of it because some people seem to be born with the gift of awareness, others recognize the value of it and spend significant seasons of their life trying to develop and grow in it—me included, and others simply do not care about or recognize the importance of this virtue.

But wherever you fall on your thoughts on awareness, I believe the ability to see or gauge how I am doing or my state of mind, how others around me are doing or their state of mind, how we are mutually impacting each other, and where God is in the spaces between us is paramount to developing a caring family.

Before I go any further, I must give credit to Steve Cuss and his teachings from *A Capable Life*.[31] Steve teaches about relationships and leading through anxiety. Steve shares about the different spaces I have mentioned. He has greatly influenced me as I have been working out my thoughts on transformational awareness. I am thankful for him.

And you may be wondering, what does Aaron mean exactly when he writes transformational awareness? I am so glad you asked! And there is no time better than now to get started.

Let's start with the awareness part first.

Awareness

I believe awareness is the ability to see or gauge how I am doing or my state of mind, how others around me are doing or their state of mind, how we are mutually impacting each other, and where God is in the spaces between us. I would like to camp here a few minutes before moving to the transformational part of the phrase.

To clarify, the seeing or gauging I am writing about when it comes to transformational awareness is not the same seeing as on the vision test I took at the DMV. I wish it was simply cut and dry like reading numbers and letters. Unfortunately, it is not.

But some of the principles from the vision test, specifically that faking it once, faking it twice, and faking it a third time can only get you so far before you are found out, do apply. I am embarrassed to admit it, but I drift and often rapidly move toward faking it when it comes to awareness. I would think by the age of forty-six, I would be past faking it, but I am not. I am still growing.

Awareness takes effort and intentionality. And if faking it does take effort and intentionality, the effort we give toward faking ultimately ends up being futile. But for some reason I frequently think that faking it will help situations or relationships turn out alright or okay. I convince myself if I can just get through the situation, it will be alright.

But as faking it on the DMV vision test eventually caught up with me, so does faking knowing how I am doing or my state of mind, knowing how others are doing or their state of mind, knowing how we are impacting each other, and knowing where God is in these spaces.

Even though I might think I am doing a good job faking awareness, those around me who are insightful and aware can easily pick up on the truth. They can see how I am doing, how others around me are doing, and how we are impacting each other. And if they are a follower of Jesus, they can see where God is in the spaces between us. They are able to see when there is something not right, even if they do not immediately know what the "not right" is. They can feel, discern, or sense it.

I think one of the reasons I turn to faking it is because I like to appear to have the right answer. As I have shared in *A Caring Life*, I have been rewarded most of my life for having the right answer. And even if I do not know the right answer for the questions about others and God, I should at least be able to respond with honesty and integrity to the question of "how are you doing?"

And similar to me giving the letter answers on the vision test that only had numbers, when I catch myself faking it when I respond to the question of "how I am doing" or "how others are doing," it is a signal that I am trying to fake my way through awareness. And a steady diet of faking it can have painful consequences for myself, those around me, and my relationship with Jesus.

But instead of heeding what my heart and mind are telling me which is to not fake it, I try to fake anyway. I choose to use information from days gone by rather than choosing courage.

In reality, being transparent about my awareness requires courage. Profound courage. And being transparent enough to share that I do not know how I am doing, how others are doing, how we are impacting each other, and where God is in the spaces is not something I share with just anyone and everyone.

I believe the family is the key for developing and modeling this type of awareness. Families can model awareness and the honesty that comes with it. Modeling awareness in the family can help family members learn to see or gauge how they are doing, others are doing, how they are impacting each other, and where God is in the spaces.

Families can model the freedom or the opportunity to share when family members do not know the answers to these questions and being able to admit when they do not know. The vulnerability it takes to admit not knowing creates an opportunity to grow together and learn from each other. By modeling this type of awareness, families are able to respond and care for themselves and others.

So what about the transformational part?

Self-Awareness Is a Start but Not Enough

After a stressful day, my family and some friends were sitting by a fire roasting some marshmallows and making s'mores. The events of the day had me irritated, frustrated, and discouraged, and I was aware of my current emotional state. But I was excited to leave that part of the day behind me and have some great conversations with friends. And in my experience, sitting by a fire and eating s'mores can make most days seem a lot better.

In the middle of roasting a marshmallow for my s'more, I heard a scream from one of my kids. Every parent knows your child's distinct scream or cry. It is one of the wonders of how God made us. A parent can be in a room with other people talking, yelling, and singing, but if your child screams or cries, it is like there is no one else in the room. And once your ears are tuned in to the scream or cry, you kick into instant action mode and try to fix what is causing your child to cry.

As I stood up and turned to look where my child's cry was coming from, I could see one of my children on the basketball court holding their mouth and could hear their cry getting louder and louder. I quickly made my way up to the basketball court where they were playing.

My other child, who had not gotten hurt, met me halfway and assured me that the hurt child would be just fine. In their opinion, the one who was hurt was overreacting. I looked over and saw blood on the face of the child who was hurt, so I was not yet convinced they were overreacting. Through their sobs and blood, my child shared they had knocked their tooth out when they ran blindfolded into a basketball backboard support pole. Metal wins over teeth most times.

Remaining calm was getting harder to do, but I was trying. I was aware of how I was feeling. I was telling myself "younger kids lose their baby teeth all the time." I was just thankful that it was not an adult permanent tooth. Until my child opened their mouth and I realized it was an adult tooth, the front adult tooth, the one we had been waiting for months to come in. It had broken off where it met the gum line.

I would love to tell you that my awareness of how I was doing, how my kids were doing, how we were impacting each other, and where God was in this space guided my responses. And I avoided being frustrated, irritated, and discouraged and pushed through and responded with love and compassion. With great understanding and care, I embraced my child and told them it would be okay.

But this type of response was exactly the opposite of what I did. I began to shout to my wife to come quickly because one of our kids had knocked out their permanent front tooth. And my response to the situation went downhill from there. Until, that is, I looked at my child and recognized that they were now getting more upset because of me and how I was responding. My awareness was not impacting my actions and influencing how I was caring for them.

The discouraging part of this was before the tooth incident, I had put a ton of time and effort into becoming more aware of myself and how I impacted others. I had listened to more Focus on the Family podcasts than you could count. I was learning to examine how I was doing inwardly and trying to use words to describe my feelings and emotions. And that day I realized that just being aware was not good enough because being only aware did not change my actions, and being only aware did not help my child who I was caring for.

Steve Cuss and his teachings through *A Capable Life* have helped me understand that awareness is only part of my challenge, and being aware is not really my goal.[31] Steve eloquently shares that transformation is the goal. And this so truly resonates with me.

You see, I was aware that I was frustrated, irritated, and discouraged, but when it came to caring for my child who was hurt, those things still spilled out. If I was using my awareness skills and had been transformed, I would have been, as Steve shares, calm, aware, and present. And when we are calm, aware, and present, we are able to be the parent and family member we desire to be and the one that is able to care for ourselves and others.

That evening I had a lot of apologizing to do, first to my child who was hurt, then to my wife and other child who got unfairly caught in my frustration, and finally to my friends with whom we were roasting marshmallows.

As parents, we have the opportunity to instill the virtue of awareness that leads to transformation, a transformational awareness which helps them remain calm, aware, and present. When we are able to do this, we are laying the foundation for our family to become better equipped at caring for others and responding with love and compassion when they are confronted with or given the opportunity to care for themselves and others during challenging times.

Other Awareness

I have found that one of the most caring things a person can do to show that they are others-aware is to sincerely apologize when they have said or done something, intentionally or unintentionally, to hurt someone else. I regret that I did not demonstrate or model the art of an apology to my children when they were younger.

To apologize is to recognize that we impact each other, and sometimes our impact can be hurtful and painful, leaving ripples and a wake behind us long after we have passed through. Mark Batterson does a phenomenal job sharing the power of the word "sorry" in his book.[32]

Sincere Apology

Although I regret not modeling the power of sorry and the art of an apology, some believe that a sincere apology is a sign of weakness and avoid apologizing at all costs. And in refusing to apologize they continue to heap hurt onto hurt and outwardly demonstrate their inner feelings and show their deficiency in being others-aware.

In contrast to seeing a sincere apology as weakness, I believe that a sincere apology is a very courageous act because it requires humility and vulnerability, and both of these require deep courage and rich inner strength. Once again, if you have not read it yet, Batterson's book is excellent.[32]

You may be wondering why I keep writing "sincere apology." It is because I differentiate a sincere apology from going through the motions and saying a set of words. These types of apologies are not others-aware and are more about the person who has brought hurt to others rather than a humble and vulnerable admission that you have caused hurt and pain.

A sincere apology is not saying what needs to be said so you can move on or move past what has happened and relieve your conscience. It is when the person who has hurt someone takes responsibility for their words and actions, with no pressure placed on the person who has been hurt to forgive them or restore the relationship to where it previously was.

And I believe the family is the best place for children to see and experience sincere apologies modeled and demonstrated. Parents and family members can set the course for being a caring family who is others-aware by modeling the art of a sincere apology both inwardly and outwardly, inwardly toward each other and outwardly to those outside the family. One thing about living in close proximity to others is it gives you ample opportunities to grow in how you apologize.

Andy Stanley recently shared a series of messages on "The Weight of Our Words," and in this series he gave some practical tips on the art of an apology.[30] The series provided a broad discussion on the power of our words, but the message on apologizing has truly impacted me. Here are a few things he shared that I wish I would have been more intentional about when my kids were at home to help model others awareness.

The first thing that Stanley shared was that an apology combined with an explanation often comes across as trying to shift the blame away from the one apologizing onto something or someone else.[30] When you or I apologize and then try to explain our actions and words, we can end up inflicting more pain and hurt rather than being humble and vulnerable. An apology that was given to provide the possibility for healing and restoration can end up inflicting more pain. When we take responsibility for what we have said or done, an apology is powerful.

Stanley also highlighted that when we try to explain the reason behind what we have said or done, the person we have hurt can feel like we are trying to force them to forget it.[30] Forgive me. And move on. Rather, we should be willing to be calm, aware, and present as Steve Cuss shares, and be open to hearing from them about the impact we have had on them.[31]

The next thing that Stanley shared was that when we apologize, we need to begin the apology with "I" and end the apology with "sorry for what I said or did." The apology should sound like this, "I am so sorry for . . ." It is valuable to use specific words that acknowledge the hurt we have caused and the impact it has made on the person to whom we are apologizing. And once we have shared that we are sorry, we keep our mouth shut—my words, not his. He is a far better communicator than I am.

Stanley shares that anything after the "I am so sorry for . . ." feels like deflection, blame, and an excuse. If we continue to talk after apologizing, it becomes more about the one who has caused the hurt trying to be understood and justified rather than being humble and vulnerable. Stanley shares that "the one apologizing needs to sit in their guilt while the person who has been hurt sits in their pain."[30]

A Summer Lesson

The summer after graduating and before entering nursing school, I took a job in a German restaurant as a dishwasher. My parents were not excited about me taking the job, because of the road I would need to drive back and forth on to and from work. But I wanted a job to begin saving money for college, this one presented itself, so I took it. It was hard, sweaty work, but I was able to do it with great people, which made it fun.

One afternoon on the way to work, I was driving the best of the two family cars we had when the traffic dramatically came to a screeching halt. My reflexes were not quick enough, and I remember slamming on the breaks so hard that I lifted myself up off the seat even though I was wearing my seatbelt. Although I tried, I did not get stopped fast enough and ran into the rear end of the car in front of me.

To my surprise, the car I hit was full of teenagers about my age. But they did not get out of their car or stay at the scene of the accident. They quickly drove off. I was shaken and did not know what to do.

After looking my car over and assessing the damage, I realized it was still drivable. I received a few one-finger gestures from those forced to go around me because I was still in the middle of the road. Eventually, I got the point and drove my dad's smashed car and my damaged ego to the state police barracks to report what had happened.

When I arrived, the state police said someone had just called in and shared they had been rear ended by a driver in a stolen car. The caller communicated they were afraid to stay at the scene because the driver of the car that hit them looked menacing. So, they left the scene to avoid getting hurt by the menacing driver.

Through my years, I have been accused of many things, but mean and menacing are not two of them. Coincidentally, and over a series of conversations in the months that followed, I came to find out that the passengers in the car I had rear ended had drugs in their car and did not want to stay at the scene because they were afraid they would be caught.

It did not make a difference what I found out months later or that they left the scene of the accident because the state police stated I had hit them from the rear, so I was responsible. I knew that to be true, but I was devastated nonetheless. When I pulled myself together, I continued on to work lamenting the damage that was done to my dad's car and wondering how my parents would respond to what had happened.

I could not keep the news of what had happened to myself for the six-hour shift, so I called my parents and told them what happened. My dad calmly said we would talk about it when I got home. But as I washed the dishes that night, I ran the accident over and over in my mind. I was devastated that I had wrecked the family car and had no idea how I would pay to have it repaired.

When I arrived home that night, I was expecting my dad to be upset and angry. The best car our family had was now damaged and it was my fault. And I will never forget his response. Honestly, I never will.

My dad looked at me and put his arm around me and said, "Hey, I got a call from the local race track this evening and they are looking for drivers for the crash up derby. Are you interested?" And then he smiled.

I was shocked by his response and his awareness of how I was feeling. He did not pile onto my despair as he could have and had every right to do. He chose to not second guess what I could have done differently to avoid the accident. He chose transformational awareness. That transformed me.

That evening he told me that we would sleep on it and figure out what to do in the morning. And we did. The power of a good night's sleep.

Through transformational awareness of others, my dad helped me learn to take responsibility for my actions. I went to the insurance company and came up with a plan on how I would pay to have the car repaired through my dishwashing job. That summer I learned a few lessons like growing up, taking responsibility, and that my dad loved me more than any possession he had.

But the biggest lesson I learned that summer was one of transformational awareness. My father's awareness transformed me. It transformed my understanding on how to respond to others who have made a mistake. When others make a mistake that ultimately impacts me, I do not need to pile on. He taught me to focus on the person and let the rest take care of itself. That is transformational awareness.

Cultural Awareness

Guiding and modeling what cultural awareness looks like can be uncomfortable. It can feel awkward at first. And if you are looking for the easiest virtue for your family to practice, caring cross-culturally will not top the easy list. It is hard. It can be complex and takes time, energy, and prayer. Cultural awareness requires a humble and open heart.

If you desire for your family to be a caring family, learning to become culturally aware is vital. And if you desire for your family to care cross-culturally, you must work at helping grow the muscle that helps you push through complacency, because caring cross-culturally requires action and movement. It requires resiliency and means not giving up or giving in.

I encourage you and your family to start slowly by exploring and learning about other cultures and their different world views. Learn to ask great questions. Seek to learn about the culture before jumping in doing something. And once you take the leap to start caring cross-culturally, build off of your wins. Because not all your attempts to care cross-culturally will be wins. But celebrate the ones that are and use those wins as inspiration to continue forward.

I have shared earlier about the virtue of courage that is needed to have a caring family. Often today, lack of courage is what hinders families from becoming culturally aware and caring cross-culturally. Many of us do not begin caring from a place of courage, but rather from a place of fear. The close cousin to complacency (the big enemy) and apathy is fear. It will be challenging, at best, to care for someone from another culture, another worldview, and another perspective in life if paralyzed by fear. But I believe courageous, caring families can do it.

As a parent, I have tried finding courage to help me grow in cultural awareness so I could model it in my family. Growing up in Wiley Ford, West Virginia, gave me many things but cultural awareness was not one of them. I have tried more education, asking better questions, increasing my language capabilities, and seeking out cultural guides.

All have been valuable, while at the same time not enough to dispel my fears and take away the intimidation of caring for others who do not look, sound, dress, or think like me. The only thing I have found that has provided true courage to become more culturally aware is my relationship with Jesus. To care cross-culturally you must have courage which comes from Him.

Being culturally aware also means your family will need to develop toughness and have a high tolerance for questions, doubts, and suspicions. Those close to your family may criticize your family for caring for someone who is different than you are. Others may question and doubt your motives, and people may be suspicious of your true intentions.

I cannot count how many times someone has questioned me personally. From the woman in a rural area chewing me out for holding a clinic in the village with the intention of stealing the teenage girls, or the Chinese businessman living in another town where we conducted a medical clinic accusing me of being a CIA spy. I had a genuine desire to care for others who did not look like me, live like me, act like me, or see the world as I saw it, only for that care to get lost in the cultural differences between myself and them.

But I was hesitant and missed opportunities to model caring cross-culturally because of my concern for my family. Subjecting myself was one thing, but signing them up also was something I struggled with.

Leadership consultant and author T. J. Addington says living a life with nothing to prove and nothing to lose is extremely valuable.[33] This has become my go-to phrase when my motives are questioned or when someone is suspicious of me. I simply say to myself, "I have nothing to prove and nothing to lose." I wish I would have taken this approach more frequently and demonstrated it to my family.

My main struggle was that I wanted to control outcomes and when the outcomes were not what I wanted, I was frustrated. When I let go of controlling and took on the "nothing to prove or lose" mentality, caring cross-culturally was purer and richer, and less baffling.

If you desire to care cross-culturally, resisting complacency, being of great courage, and having a "nothing to prove, nothing to lose" attitude is a great foundation from which to build. The characteristics of being flexible, adaptable, and humble are solid building blocks from which to build a cross-cultural caring family.

God Aware

Recognizing God's presence in our everyday lives is foundational for life and essential for a caring family in their development of transformational awareness. If we are self-aware, others-aware, aware about how we are impacting each other, culturally aware, and forget to be God aware, we have missed the centerpiece of transformational awareness. It is truly He who does the transforming in and through us. Acknowledging His presence helps us pause and ponder where He is in the space we are in.

My wife has often reminded me and put it on our refrigerator, lest I forget, that wherever we are is a place God is and has been. She also shares that wherever we will go is a place God has already been.

Although these two ideas may seem simple to you, they have been profound for me as I have grown in my God awareness. I have spent significant time considering how it is ultimately Him who gives me the strength to care for others and the insight to where God was in some of the most joyous and challenging times of my life.

One of the times that he protected me was when I was growing up. When I was a kid, I had a great desire to be a professional basketball player. I had the heart and passion, but not the height, length, speed, or quickness. But I did not know all of my weaknesses when I was younger and my dreams were still alive. I loved playing basketball and took any and every opportunity I could get to play the game I loved.

Even though I grew up in a really small town, the largest town nearest to mine was still not very big. But every year, it hosted a high school basketball tournament—The Alhambra Catholic Invitational Tournament (ACIT). Some of the powerhouse catholic high schools from the East Coast would often venture in the month of March to the mountains of Western Maryland to compete in the tournament. The tournament put a buzz in the air and renewed my passion to practice basketball so that one day I could play in a similar tournament.

One day, my friends and I were playing basketball on the elementary school playground. As always, competition was high, and emotions ran higher. We used our best moves and formed the best teams so we could stay on the court the longest. But on this Saturday, our luck was even greater. Or so we thought.

This Saturday, a man unknown to us showed up at the playground. He was tall and athletic looking and shared that he was visiting local playgrounds looking for talent. Maybe he thought he was going to find the next great West Virginia basketball player like Jerry West. Who knows.

He also shared that he represented the Boston Celtics as a scout and was in town to watch the ACIT. It made sense to our young minds. And so my friends and I played our hearts out trying to impress this man. I honestly thought that this was an answer to my prayers to become a professional player. That a scout for the Boston Celtics had shown up in Wiley Ford, WV, was a true miracle. My heart was full of excitement and anticipation.

And then I heard the sound that no kid wants to hear when they are in the middle of their audition for the Boston Celtics—a mother's voice calling you to come home. I tried to ignore the voice and convince myself that it was not my mom. It had to be someone else's mom. But even though I tried to convince myself otherwise, I finally relented and made my way home.

As I entered our house, I shared my frustration and irritation with my mom. I explained to her how she had just ruined my chances of ever playing for the Boston Celtics. My mom laughed and was in disbelief that there would be a scout for the Celtics in our small town.

I asked her the age-old question that most kids try when they want to get their way: "Why?" Why did I need to come home? Why did she not believe there was a Boston Celtic scout in our neighborhood? She did not have much of an explanation other than she sensed that I needed to come home. I pushed back a little and wanted to return to the court, but she would not change her mind. I was staying home.

My mom has great God awareness and is sensitive to his voice and his leading. And that day, her sensitivity to where God was and what He was telling her saved me from danger.

I stayed at home the rest of that day. I pouted around thinking of the missed opportunity and the frustration with a mother who did not understand the importance of my opportunity to impress this scout.

The next day at church I was talking to some friends and quickly realized how my mom's God awareness saved me. My friends who lived in a nearby town were talking about the same basketball scout who had visited our playground.

The supposed scout for the Boston Celtics ended up at a playground in their neighborhood. He had convinced another young kid to get into the car with him and had some very bad intentions of what he was going to do to this young kid. My mom's voice and recognition of where God was and her obedience to what He was telling her saved me that day. If not, I would have probably done whatever that man said just like the other kid had done because I believed what the man was telling us.

My wife, Heather, has also started encouraging me to begin to ask the question, "Where is Jesus in this story?" And asking this question has made me so much more aware of His presence and how His presence can bring transformation. But unfortunately, this question was not something that I asked my kids when they were growing up.

And by not asking this question of "where is Jesus in your story or life," I missed a rich opportunity to help them grow further and deeper in understanding God's presence in everyday situations of life. I now wish that it was a skill that I taught or modeled in my family. But the good part is it is never too late to start. And I encourage you to start asking the question in your family today.

A Caring Family

As I mentioned in the opening of this chapter, if awareness was just as easy as getting a set of glasses that could correct any discrepancies in how we perceive ourselves, how we perceive others, how we recognize the dynamics between ourselves and others, and help us see where God is in the spaces between us, awareness would be common. Unfortunately, awareness is not common in the self-focused world we live in. But caring families know that transformational awareness impacts and guides how their mindset impacts others and helps them care for others during their times of need.

Transformational awareness helps a family care in deep and rich ways. Its value cannot be understated for families who desire to grow in how they care for others. I would encourage you to consider these questions yourself and then discuss them in an age-appropriate way with your family.

Transformational Awareness

1. What are some reasons you think it is valuable to move beyond just awareness?

2. How can you lead your family to grow both in awareness of others and transformation and growth?
3. How can you as a parent be transparent about learning and growing? How is that more impactful than trying to fake it?

Self-Awareness Is a Start but Not Enough
1. How do you define self-awareness?
2. What are some ways you can become more self-aware?
3. Who are people in your life that could help you answer the question, "What is it like being on the other side of me?"

Other Awareness
1. How does apologizing show other awareness?
2. Does apologizing flow naturally within your family?
3. As a parent, do you model apologizing to you children when you have made a mistake?

Cultural Awareness
1. Do you enjoy learning about other cultures?
2. How does cultural awareness impact how you care for others?
3. What are some ways you can model perseverance in becoming culturally aware?

God Aware
1. Are you able to recognize God's hand in everyday situations?
2. Have you ever asked, "Where is Jesus at?" in this caring opportunity? What are some reasons this is an important question?

3. How can you model God's awareness in your family?

CONCLUSION

Congratulations! You survived my stories and are still reading!

Family is often where caring is learned, ideas are formulated, connections are made, and where we begin testing and experimenting with caring for others. And I am more and more convinced that how our acts and concepts of caring are received and acknowledged orients our trajectory for the future of each of our caring lives. Our family life, for better or worse, impacts how we see the world and those around us and our willingness to care for them.

An intentional way of family life that centers around the seven virtues you have read on these pages is essential for *A Caring Family*. Loyalty, Courage, Resiliency, Emotional Honesty, Spiritually Focused, Patience, and Transformational Awareness are the virtues that I wish I had more intentionally focused on while Heather and I were raising our kids. I would have valued someone sitting me down twenty years ago and having the discussion that I have shared in this book. In a way, this is a book to my younger self, but unfortunately, I cannot relive or change the past. But the good thing is that you can benefit from the lessons I have learned the hard way.

Loyalty: the virtue that provides stability—The importance of the virtue of loyalty in a caring family cannot be overstated. Parents, grandparents, aunts, uncles, and other family members have the opportunity to model and demonstrate what true loyalty looks like. But families will need to push back against our current culture which has shifted the definition of the word loyalty from an inner motivation that is predicated on moral courage to more of a transactional term where loyalty is based upon a mutually beneficial situation. Families also need to model that loyalty does not mean walking away when the mutual benefit deteriorates or becomes inconvenient but stays and cares.

Emotional Honesty: the virtue that provides understanding— Emotional honesty is a vital virtue for a caring family. God created us with emotions and feelings as ways of sending signals and communicating to ourselves and others. But oftentimes, our lack of a clear understanding of what emotions and feelings are can leave us wondering how to understand what they are communicating to us and others. Add to this a feeling of being uncomfortable with feelings of hurt, lonely, sad, anger, fear, shame, and guilt, we can drift toward not wanting to care for others experiencing these feelings. Families that provide a safe space for each other to share, in a respectful and loving way, their emotions and feelings help build a solid foundation for caring for others.

Courage: the virtue that provides strength—Caring for others requires great courage. Without courage, we can often surrender to fear that moves us toward self rather than others. Stephen Blandino lists common fears as fear of failure, rejection, lack, criticism, communication, decision-making, inadequacy, risk-taking, standing up, and significance. Courage is not the absence of these fears but pushing through them to care for others. The family provides a safe place for family members to experience caring for others with the support and strength provided by other family members.

Resiliency: the virtue that provides a new normal—Being able to bounce back from difficult life events and stressful experiences to a new normal is a skill and a blessing that can be demonstrated and modeled in the home. Resiliency is paramount for caring families, and parents can provide intentional opportunities in caring to help their children grow this resiliency muscle. When faced with predictable roadblocks and obstacles like disorientation, doubt, discouragement, and dissonance, parents can model the positive antidotes that can be used against these. If children are given the opportunity to develop antidotes early on, it will help them move through these common obstacles, continue to care, and arrive at a new normal.

Spiritually focused: the virtue that provides hope and creativity—We are spiritual beings with a past, present, and eternal future. And caring is a truly spiritual act. Parents have the space and time to help their children learn to hear God's voice and learn to follow what He is saying. Recognizing that God is nearer than we think, He wants to speak to us and is interested in our everyday lives and the lives of others, He will not compete for our attention so we need to provide space for Him to speak and for us to listen, and that He wants to show up in our lives should encourage us to be more interested in listening to Him. Healthy families provide fertile ground for children to hear God's voice and be guided in obeying it.

Patience: the virtue that provides perspective—Some might consider patience to be an old-fashioned virtue, but it is highly valued and produces exceptional fruit in our lives. Patience offers fruits like maturity and wisdom, healthier relationships, higher quality work, and peace of mind. Although it produces the fruit many desire in their lives, developing this virtue in an instant society and fast-paced world can be challenging. If we desire to have a caring family, patience is a must. Families that are driven by action and do not set aside time to listen to others will need to slow down and learn that waiting is an action verb. And when families demonstrate having more time and space and truly listening to others, they will see that patience truly makes them more of a caring family.

Transformational Awareness: the virtue that provides growth and change—If awareness was just as easy as getting a set of glasses that could correct any discrepancies in how we perceive ourselves, how we perceive others, how we recognize the dynamics between ourselves and others, and help us see where God is in the spaces between us, awareness would be common. Adding to this, a caring family does not have awareness as its ultimate goal but wants to see transformation take place. Caring families know that transformational awareness impacts and guides how their mindset impacts others and helps them care for others during their times of need. Inevitably, caring families will not get it right every time, and that is why the art of a sincere apology is something families can model and demonstrate so that they are able to express themselves when they have not hit the mark.

My hope is that through all the storytelling and discussion of these seven virtues you and your family can begin to discuss, model, and emulate what a caring family looks, sounds, and acts like. Our world is desperately in need of families that prioritize caring for themselves and others, changing one life at a time. And by growing as a caring family, you will demonstrate that people belong, matter, and are known. What will your *caring family* look like and whose lives will you impact? I am excited to hear of the lives that will be changed because you have chosen to be a caring family.

ACKNOWLEDGMENTS

To My Family

I am blessed with a phenomenal supportive family who has encouraged me through the ups and downs of writing this book. Your encouragement, patience, and belief in my writing are a blessing. Heather, Isabelle and Josiah, thank you for encouraging me to chase my dreams and loving me along the way. Dad, thanks for loving me and taking me on adventures so I could have great storytelling material. Mom, even though you passed before this book was published, you cheered me on during the early days of writing it and helped reel me in on some of my tall tales in storytelling. Beth and Carissa, I love you both. Lilly, Zechariah, and Ella, dream big dreams and eat broccoli ice cream.

To Walker

My heartfelt thanks go to Walker Kuykendall. You provided a sharp eye, valuable feedback, and commitment to polishing my West Virginia grammar so this book could be readable, compelling, and cohesive. Your editorial expertise is a blessing. You have a gift.

To Morgan James

David Hancock, thank you for believing in me and my desire to encourage families. Les Hughes and EntrePastors, thank you for connecting me with David and supporting me in this process. Gayle West, thank you for being my author relations manager and guiding me on my publishing journey.

To Readers

I write so that you can do exceedingly better than I have. Your life and the lives you care for, matter beyond measure, forever.

To Jesus

May I glorify You in all I do.

ABOUT THE AUTHOR

Aaron is a husband, father, nurse practitioner, host of *The Clarity Podcast*, and, most importantly, a follower of Jesus. He is from the "almost heaven" state of West Virginia and has a Doctor of Nursing Practice from West Virginia University, an MBA from Southwestern Assemblies of God University, and a Bachelor of Arts in Bible and Missions from Southeastern University. Aaron has spent the last twenty years of his life serving in Africa, specifically Burkina Faso, Madagascar, and Kenya. He loves to fish for trout, eat homemade apple pie, talk to his orchids, and cheer on the West Virginia Mountaineers.

ENDNOTES

1. Campbell, Reggie. *Radical Wisdom.* iDisciple Publishing, 2018.

2. Dobson, James. "Setting Right Parental Missteps" One Place, https://www.oneplace.com/ministries/family-talk/read/articles/setting-right-parental-missteps-15006.html. 3 August 2023.

3. Leman, Kevin, guest. *Raising Well Behaved Children.* 1 March 2023. March 2023. <https://www.focusonthefamily.com/episodes/broadcast/game-plan-for-raising-well-behaved-children-part-1-of-2/.>.

4. Ingram, Chip. "Living on the Edge." 3 August 2020. *Living on the Edge.* August 2023. <https://messagenotes.livingontheedge.org/Trusting-Jesus-No-Matter-What.pdf>.

5. Brooks, Arthur. *From Strength to Strength: Finding Success and Happiness in the Second Half of Life.* Green Tree Publishing, 2023.

6. Brown, James. *Boys in the Boat.* Penguin, 2013.

7. Royal Rangers. "Royal Rangers Program." *Activity based small group program church ministry for young men.* n.d.

8. McKnight, S and L Barringer. *A Church Called Tov: Forming a Goodness Culture that Resists Abuses of Power and Promotes Healing.* Tyndale Elevate, 2020.

9. Langer, R and J Jung. *The Call to Follow: Hearing Jesus in a Culture Obsessed with Leadership.* Crossway, 2022.

10. McKnight, Scot. "The Church Called Tov." *The Clarity Podcast.* Aaron Santmyire. The Clarity Podcast, 19 March 2023.

11. Jenner, Nicholas. "The Online Therapist." 12 July 2018. *theonlinetherapist.* July 2022. <https://theonlinetherapist.blog/emotional-honesty-what-it-is-and-why-it-is-important/>.

12. Dodd, Chip. *Voices of the Heart: A Call to Full Living.* Sage Hill Publishers, 2015.

13. Farina, Sam. "Building Teams." *The Clarity Podcast.* Aaron Santmyire. 18 February 2020.

14. Ulrika, Ernvik. *Third Culture Kids: A Gift to Care For.* Familjeglädje, 2019.

15. Wells, Lauren. *Raising a Healthy Generation of Third Culture Kids: A Practical Guide to Preventative Care.* Independent, 2020.

16. Lowe, Ted. *Us in Mind: How Changing Your Thoughts Can Change Your Marriage*. Orange, 2022.

17. David, Susan. *Emotional Agility: Get Unstuck, Embrace Change, and Thrive in Work and Life*. Avery, 2016.

18. Nieuwhof, Toni. *Before you Split: Find What you Really Want for the Future of your Marriage*. Waterbrook, 2021.

19. Neuroqualia. The Human Affectome Project. http://www. neuroqualia.org. Accessed 19 May 2023.

20. Davis, Nathan and B Davis. *Resilience. Skills for global servants*. Assemblies of God World Missions, 2010.

21. Cloud, Henry. *Trust: Knowing When to Give It, When to Withhold It, How to Earn It, and How to Fix It When It is Broken*. Worthy Books, 2023.

22. Blandino, Stephen. "Leading Through Fear." *The Clarity Podcast*. Aaron Santmyire. 23 March 2023.

23. Frey, Butch. "Resilience." Cape Town, 26 April 2023. Personal Communication.

24. Gordon, Jon. *The Garden. A Spiritual Fable about the Ways to Overcome Fear, Anxiety, and Stress*. Wiley, 2020.

25. Gordon, Jon. "The Garden." *The Clarity Podcast*. Aaron Santmyire. The Clarity Podcast, 8 January 2023.

26. YouVersion. New International Version, app version 9.3.3. Life Church. 2023.

27. Elsey, E.L. *The Coaching Tools Company*. 15 December 2021. February 2023. <https://www.thecoachingtoolscompany.com/think-acronym-for-kinder-and-more-effective-communications/>.

28. Ingram, Ryan. "When We Pray: Hearing God." *Living on the Edge Podcast*. Unknown: Living on the Edge, 18 May 2023. Podcast.

29. Ryan, M.J. *The Power of Patience: How this Old Fashioned Virtue can Improve your Life*. Conari, 2022.

30. Stanley, Andy. "Weight of Your Words." *North Point Community Podcast*. North Point, 20 February 2023. Podcast.

31. Cuss, Steve. *A Capable Life*. 15 April 2022. May 2023. <https://capablelife.me>.

32. Batterson, Mark. *Please, Sorry, Thanks: Three Words That Change Everything*. Multnomah, 2023.

33. Addington, T.J. *Deep Influence: Unseen Practices That Will Revolutionize Your Leadership*. NavPress, 2014.

A free ebook edition is available with the purchase of this book.

To claim your free ebook edition:

1. Visit MorganJamesBOGO.com
2. Sign your name CLEARLY in the space
3. Complete the form and submit a photo of the entire copyright page
4. You or your friend can download the ebook to your preferred device

Morgan James BOGO™

A **FREE** ebook edition is available for you or a friend with the purchase of this print book.

CLEARLY SIGN YOUR NAME ABOVE

Instructions to claim your free ebook edition:
1. Visit MorganJamesBOGO.com
2. Sign your name CLEARLY in the space above
3. Complete the form and submit a photo of this entire page
4. You or your friend can download the ebook to your preferred device

Print & Digital Together Forever.

Snap a photo

Free ebook

Read anywhere